John Payne Collier, Thomas Richards

Broadside Black-Letter Ballads

Printed in the sixteenth and seventeenth centuries

John Payne Collier, Thomas Richards

Broadside Black-Letter Ballads
Printed in the sixteenth and seventeenth centuries

ISBN/EAN: 9783744796446

Printed in Europe, USA, Canada, Australia, Japan

Cover: Foto ©Thomas Meinert / pixelio.de

More available books at **www.hansebooks.com**

BROADSIDE
𝔅lack=letter 𝔅allads,

PRINTED IN THE

SIXTEENTH AND SEVENTEENTH CENTURIES;

CHIEFLY IN THE POSSESSION OF

J. PAYNE COLLIER.

ILLUSTRATED BY

Original Woodcuts.

PRINTED (FOR PRIVATE CIRCULATION)
BY THOMAS RICHARDS.
1868.

TO

FREDERIC OUVRY, ESQ.,

TREASURER OF THE SOCIETY OF ANTIQUARIES,
LONDON,

THIS TRIFLING TRIBUTE OF HIGH RESPECT
AND SINCERE AFFECTION

IS DEDICATED BY

J. PAYNE COLLIER.

Maidenhead,
11 *Jan.* 1868.

All the poems, so to call them, are of my own composition.

Maidenhead
11 Jan 1870

My dear Sir

I thank you for accepting my trifling book. There are a few good things in it — I am bound to say.

Thank you also for the P. O. Order. Your name is on my list for my <u>Blue</u> Series.

Yours very faithfully
J. Payne Collier

J Symes Saunders Esq.

PREFACE.

THE greater number of Ballads in the enſuing ſmall aſſemblage is from the editor's collection: one or two have been derived from other private ſources, and perhaps, as many from manuſcript copies made forty, or even fifty, years ago. It will be found that they all poſſeſs ſome features of intereſt, while only a few, it muſt be owned, are worthy of preſervation for their own ſeparate and poetical merits. Moſt of them are unique, but two may be looked upon as unknown ſecond editions of popular productions, which had juſt previouſly appeared. Others eſtabliſh the fact that our old ſtationers, now and then, reſorted for attractive broadſides to works of a more permanent deſcription.

Twenty years ſince, in the introduction to a volume called "A Book of Roxburghe Ballads," the preſent editor entered tolerably fully into the origin and pro-

PREFACE.

greſs of what may be called ſtreet-ballad-literature in this country. He has now little to add to that eſſay, which ſhowed that public ballad-ſinging was well received and underſtood about the middle of the reign of Henry VIII; but the following woodcut, derived from Caxton's "Mirror of the World," which obviouſly repreſents two ſtreet-performers, male and female, one ſinging and the other playing, may carry us back at least to the year 1481.

It would not, we think, be difficult to eſtabliſh that

such performances commenced with the commencement of our popular lyrical poetry. Upon this point it is not our purpose here to enlarge; but, coming down to the reign of Philip and Mary, we may note that our statute-book contains evidence that the public authorities of that day took vigorous measures to restrain or suppress ballad-printing and ballad-singing, as objectionable upon both religious and political considerations.

Our series, if such it can be called, begins at about this period, although it comprises no specimen of precisely that kind: our first and second pieces are merely love-poems, our third is purely religious, and our fourth social, political and religious: if we mistake not, it is one of the most singular early lyrical satires in our language; and being found only at Lambeth, it is not unlikely that it was forbidden by the archbishop and other persons connected with the government, although still preserved in the library The figure of R. Copland, the printer, which we have placed at the end of it, was his own representation of his personal appearance, prefixed to one of the works issued from his press. It is not, however, our intention here to notice other peculiarities belonging to productions in the hands of the reader, becaufe in our brief notes, at the clofe, we have, we hope, given all neceffary information. It would have been eafy to have drawn out this part of our fmall volume to any undefirable extent; but our intention was to render the notes as fhort, and yet as fatisfactory, as poffible. We have no room, and our readers, we apprehend, as little patience, for what is merely fpeculative and conjectural.

Our imitative woodcuts, we at once admit, have this defect—that although there is not one that is not derived from fome old ballad in our poffeffion, they are not fo ftrictly adapted to the places where they are found as we at firft intended. Our early printers of this ephemeral fpecies of literature may be faid to have been themfelves regardlefs of the applicability of their engravings: all they ufually wanted was fome attractive reprefentation or ornament; and for this purpofe publifhers, like Lacy, Aldee, Symcocke, Trundle and the Goffons, were in the habit of buying up coarfe worn-out, and worm-eaten woodcuts, and putting them at the head of any broadfide they would fit. The comparatively fmall fize of our page has fometimes unwillingly prevented us from following, in this refpect, the example of our predeceffors, so as to give exact repetitions; but wherever it could be accomplifhed we have not neglected this point; and it now and then feems to have happened, as regards the portraits of traitors and malefactors, that the original printers of broadfides went to the expenfe of engraving a likenefs of the party executed. In thefe cafes we have fcrupuloufly adhered to their method, and, as to all the reft, we have inferted nothing that is not warranted by fome fimilar publication of the time, and which had been repeatedly employed for the purpofe: thus, the fhip, on the forefront of the ballad celebrating the capture of "the great Galeazzo," p. 79, is found at the head of other broadfides, as well as on the title-pages of fome pamphlets, fuch, for inftance, as Smith's "True Relation of Virginia," 4to. 1608. The woodcut on p. 63 belonged originally to Fox's "Martyrs," but was afterwards made applicable to executions by fire.

As a ftriking proof of the inattention by old printers to relationfhip between letter-prefs and woodcuts, we may ftate that the fubfequent excellent and characteriftic defign, about the year 1650, was

made by Harper to introduce a tender Dialogue on the parting of two Lovers.

If the above engraving had been placed at the head of any fong upon, or againſt, drinking, it would not have feemed fo outragiouſly inappropriate; and in 1635 Raworth very properly made it the centre of the title-page of T. Heywood's "Philocothoniſta, or the Drunkard opened, diſſected and anatomiſed."

The excellent and liberal manner in which Mr. Huth has recently made his vaſt ſtore of ballads acceſſible to the Philobiblon Society, unqueſtionably inſtigated the preſent editor to purſue a ſomewhat ſimilar method with his very inſignificant, yet ſomewhat peculiar, acquiſitions of the like kind. He had originally intended to extend his ſeries from 1550 to 1660; but the expenſe of his undertaking has exceeded his calculation, and he is thereby induced to poſtpone the completion of his purpoſe to a future opportunity.

Here the editor had intended to conclude his preface, but accidentally finding, among his forgotten papers, a few curious memoranda regarding ballad-writers, bookſellers, and printers, derived from the Regiſters of the Stationers' Company (which he carefully examined more than twenty years ago) he could not reſiſt the temptation of appending them. It will be ſeen that the information, though ſcanty, (and never till now noticed) is entirely miſcellaneous, and is ſcattered through the volumes without much connexion or any regularity. There feems a long interval between 1580 and 1594, regarding which we poffefs little or no information; but it was, neverthelefs, a period during which the production, purchafe, and performance of ftreet-ballads were continued with unabated diligence and eagernefs.

15 Junij 1578.

Ric. Jones. Received of him for printing two ballades, viz. *Faythe, ye lie*, and *In unwritten bookes.* 2s.
Received of him for *Certen newes of the Prynce of Parma*, 6d.

2 Die Augufti 1578.

John Aldee. He is fined, at a Court holden the daye aforefaid, to paye 5s. for printing 3 ballads for Edward White, and *Mundaies Dreame* for himfelfe, without a lycence.

20 Sept. 1578.

Ric. Jones. He is fined to pay 5s. for printinge a booke and a ballat of *A ftraunge Dream of a Shepherd*, a ballat of *Theating of the hare*, and another, *Maydenly Counfell;* the which four thinges he printed without lycence.

Primo Die Decembr. 1578.

Jhon Charlwood. At a Court holden this day the faid Jhon Charlwood, for printinge a booke of *Fourboyfers Voiage* without lycence, is fyned to paie 5s. pd.

3 Augufti 1579.

Edward White. Received of him for printinge a ballat of *Halfpenny and Siluer*, contrary to order of this Cumpanie, 5s.

9 Aug. 1579.

Yarrath James. Roger Ward. The Court ordered Ward to pay to James 10s., to put an end to a controverfy touchinge a ballad of *Thenterteinment of the Frenchmen.*

10 Augufti 1579.

Edw. White. Receyvinge of him for printing a ballad of *Tho. Appletree* without licence xii*d*. Pd.

6 Dec. 1585.

Mr. Da[w]fon. A new order made, and entred in this booke, whereby *The Seven Sobs, The Handfull of Honey Suckles*, and *The Widows Mite*, [by W. Hunnis] are affigned to Denham, on condition that he pay £10 for the printinge of the bookes, and 40s. for his intereft in them.

7 Augufti 1592.

Whereas John Danter is appointed to print *the Instruction of a Xtian woman* and *Ovid's Metamorphofes* for the company, yt is agreed that, uppon the finifhing of thefe bookes, he fhall pay vj*d*. in the *li*. to thufe of the poore, according to order.

5º Febr. 1593.

Upon the letters of Mr. Wilbraham, yt is ordered that Toby Cooke (and none other) fhall haue the printinge of *the Truthe of the murther of Robert Hayton*, as yt fhall be found and deliuered to the faid Toby by the faid Mr. Wilbraham. And that yf any fhall prefume to meddle therewith he fhalbe ftaied.

12 May 1594.

Edw. White. At a Court holden this day it is ordered that Edward White fhall pay 5s. for a fine for printinge of a ballad of *Eating of a Sheepe* without licence, contrary to thordonances. The which he hath promifed to deliver to Mr. Warden.

iij° die Februarij 1594.

Gaul Amadis de. At a full court holden this daie, uppon the hearinge of the Controverfie betwene Adam Iflipp and Edward Aldee concerninge *the firft foure Bookes of Amadis de Gaule*, yt is ordered by this Court that the faid Adam Iflip fhall printe *the Second parte of Amadis de Gaule*. And likewife that the faid Edward Aldee fhall print *firft, third and fourthe Bookes of Amades de Gaule*. And the faid Adam to print all the reft, to the Twelfthe parte or Booke. ADAM ISLIP.
ED. ALLDE.

Tobie Cooke, Robt. Rofwell. The matter in controuerfie betwene the faid parties ys, by their confentes, referred to the hearinge and determination of Mr. John Harrifon thelder, and Mr. Watkins. And the faid parties haue agreed to ftand to their order. Memorand. that the Controuerfie is about an *Ariofto in Englifhe in Coulours*.

Primo Marcij 1595.

Abell Jeffes. To haue 2s. gyuen him who, here this day, made petition for reliefe, beinge in prifon.

10 Die Aprilis 1597.

Blackwell. William Blackwell is fyned to pay 2s. 6d. for fellinge of ballades called *Luftie Larrance*.

2 April 1598.

Adam Iflip. Received of him for printinge *The Fountaine of Fictions* without entrance.

25 Junij 1600.

Edward White, William White, Edward Aldee. Yt is ordered, touching a difordered ballad of *The Wife of Bathe*, (Percy's Reliques, edits. 1765 and 1767, vol. iii, pp. 146 and 145) printed by Edw. Aldee and William White, and fold by Edward White, that all the fame ballates fhalbe brought in and burnt, and that either of the Printers, for their diforders in printinge yt, fhall pay 5s. a pece for a fine. And that Mr. White, for his offence and diforder in felling, fhall pay 10s. for a fine. And their imprifonment is refpited.

4 Marcij 1600.

Humours Blood. Twenty-nine Stationers are fyned 6d. each for their diforders in buyinge of the bookes of *Humours letting Blood in the vayne*, being newe printed after it was firft forbydden and burnt.

23 Oct. 1600.

Ra. Blore, Wm. Jagger. They are fined vjs. viijd. for printinge, without licence and contrary to order, a little booke of *Sr. Anthony Sherleies voiage,* and bring all the copies into the hall.

1 Marcij 1601.

Ballads. Yt is ordered that all that betwene this and the next Court day bringe not in their *Ballads,* to be entred accordinge to order, ſhall loſe the ſame. And that the ſaid *Ballads* ſhalbe diſpoſed accordinge to the diſcretion of the Wardens and Aſſiſtantes.

5 Dec. 1603.

Jo. Smithick, Jo. Brown. Fined 10*s.* each for printinge a booke called *The wonderfull Yere,* without authoritie or entrance, and to bring in all copies in their hands into the Hall.

Val. Syms. An order made againſt him for *The Welch Bate,* and the ballades of *The Traitors araynned at Wincheſter.*

Meaning, of course, Lord Cobham, and Sir Walter Raleigh, for which the latter was executed fifteen years afterwards. We have no intelligence that in modern times any ſuch ballad has been diſcovered, and probably the order to Valentine Simmes againſt its publication was effectual: that there ever exiſted ſuch a production has not, we believe, been noticed by the biographers of the diſcoverer of Guiana, and the patron of Spenſer.

J. P. C.

CONTENTS.

	PAGE
Two propernue Balletes	1
Letter of a Lover	3
Prayer of the Prophet Daniel	6
New Guyse nowe a Dayes	8
Thanksgiving for the Queen	16
England's Lamentation	21
Epitaphe on Richard Goodricke	29
Cobler of Colchester	31
Ballad on Babbington, etc.	36
Fearful and Terrible Example	42
Northern Lord	48
Warning to all false Traitors	57
Lamentation of Page's Wife	63
Lamentation of G. Strangwidge	67
Complaint of Ulallia	70
Weaver's Song	73
Agincourt, the Bowman's Glory	76
Joyfull Ballad on the Galeazzo	79
The good Shepeheard	87
Salomon's Housewife	91
Story of Ill May-day	96
Desperate Damsel's Tragedy	102
Man's Creation, Adam's Fall, etc.	108
Honor of the Innes of Court	112
An excellent Medley	118

Two propernue Balletes.

————o————

. HATH my herte in holde,
So sure I can not starte,
Whiche causeth me to be bolde
With louers for to take parte.

B. hath me bounde so sure
Thorowe Venus ordynaunce,
That in paynes I must endure
There for to take my chaunce.

The paynes they be so stronge
And paynefull vnto me,
That I thynke I haue great wronge
Yf on me she haue no petie.

Nowe, petie, I the craue,
Her mynde for to remoue,
That I may ones haue
Her fauour whom I loue.

It is for no great fubftaunce,
Nor goodes that I her defyre,
But onelye for the gouernaunce,
And the honefty in her doth apere.

For yf I myght obtayne
To fall vnto my loote,
Then wolde I be moft fayne
To knyt an endles knotte.

And yf I get no grace
Of her whom I loue beft,
My herte is in a wofull cafe,
Neuer lyke for to lyue in reft.

Therfore, Venus, I the requyre,
The gods of this arte,
That foone thou wylte appere
To ftryke her with thy darte.

For to caufe her haue fome rueth,
And graunt to me her loue,
That meanes nothynge but trueth,
By God that is aboue.

Thus E., and B., I byd fare well,
Defyrynge them not to be vnkynde ;

For of letters all, both great and fmall,
They are depyſt in mynde.

Hertely vnto you I me recōmende,
Defyrynge you not to be offended,
For yf any thynge be amyſſe
That here in is,
Vnto my power it ſhalbe amended.

    My herte is yours
    Vnto the death,
    Whyle in my body
    Remaynes the breath.

FINIS.

The Letter of a Louer.

A THOUSAND times I me recomende
To you that is my louer deare,
And here a letter haue I fend,
To fpeke with you yet had I leuer.

Your luftye loke and fmerkyng chere
My hert doth moue both nyght and day:

In all thys world ye haue no pere,
Therefore to my hert I do you lay.

O lusty smyrker, to me be true:
Ye haue my hert for euer and aye.
I praye you chaunge me for no newe,
Thys same to you do I say.

I haue loued truely I dare make bost,
And doth yet styll, so god me saue:
Alas, let not my loue be lost,
But yours agayne that I may haue.

The time past I do repente,
Yf euer ye thought I was vnkinde:
To you this letter haue I sent,
Becaufe in loue I am so blynd.

The lynes of loue do me imbrase,
And bytterly beyte my body with in:
All is for your louely face
And gentyll hert, yf I myght it win.

Your countenaunce and your comely cheare,
As oft as I loke it vpon,
My hert in peces it doth teare,
When that I am my felfe alone.

The paynes of loue do me so pyne,
And perce my hert on euery syde,
That wherefoeuer I suppe or dyne,
My hert with you shall euer abyde.

The Letter of a Louer.

Alas now be a louer true,
And take neuer from me your hert,
For yf ye do I muſt it rew,
And euer lyue in payne and ſmart.

Nowe ſtedfaſt to be I do you praye,
My herte is cloſed your body within,
The fame to me nowe do you ſay:
It is trewe loue that I am in.

A thouſande tymes nowe fare you well,
Ye haue my herte both nowe and aye,
The ſorowe I byde no toung can tel:
Gentyll louer, do not caſt me awaye.

My herte is locked within your breſt,
And cloſly cloſed your body within:
There would I fayneſt take my reſte
In pure wedlocke with outten fynne.

Nowe you knowe my hole intent.
It doth me good when I you ſe:
Yf I get no grace I ſhal repent
For lokyng aboue my pore degre.
Be trewe to me in this dyſtres,
And leue me not here comfortles.

FINIS.

The prayer of the Prophet Daniel,

wrytten in the ix chapter of his Prophecie, no leſſe
Godly then neceſſary for all men at this
preſent.

Oratio Danielis, Cap. ix.

LORD, that art our God, ryght fearefull
and eke myghtie,
which euermore doſt kepe ful ſure thy coue-
naunt & thy mercie
With thē that loue the & kepe thy com-
maundemētes,
but we haue all departed from thy preceptes & judgemētes.

Ah, we haue finned, lord, and the offended fore :
we haue bene difobedient, and gone backe euermore.
We had yet neuer wyll our felfes to trade and frame
to here thy feruauntes the Prophets, whiche truly in thy name
Dyd fpeake vnto our kynges and princes through the land,
      that they fhould vnderftand
       belongth vnto thy name
       is due but open fhame
       owe at thiffame daye
       well perceyue we maye
        falem do dwell
         all Ifraell.
I meane, O lord, Jerufalem, which is thyne holy hyll,
And whye? even for our fynnes and for the wickedneffe
of oure forefathers, nowe is all this citie in diftreffe,
And we thy people all abhorred be throughout
all nacions and peoples eke, that dwell vs round about :
Nowe, therfore, O thou God of our faluacion,
heare this the prayr of thy feruaunt and fupplicacion,
And let thy face, O lord mofte glorioufe, in haft
vpon thy fanctuarye fhyne, whiche nowe lieth voyd and waft.
O lord my God, I faye, fome pitie on vs take,
inclyne thyne eare, difclofe thyne eye, at leaft for thyne owne fake.
Beholde, O lorde, howe we, confunded be with fhame,
yea, and the citie whiche alfo is called after thy name.
We do not caft our prayers, O lord, before thyne eyes,
trustyng in our owne ryghtuoufnefs, but in thy great mercies.

The Prayer of the Prophet Daniel.

O God, bowe down thyne eare; O lord, forgeue our wrong;
confidre, lord, our miseries, and tary not to long.
My God, for thyne owne sake, make haft to do the same,
for thy citie and people both be called by thyne owne name.

• *Finis orationis Danielis.*

¶ Imprinted at London in Temestrete by Hughe Syngelton, at the sygne of the dobbell hood, ouer agaynst the Stylyard.

The new guyse nowe a Dayes.

———o———

E Englishmen, that holde
   Our auncient customes olde
   More precious then golde,
     Be cleane cast away;
   And other new be fand,
Which, ye may vnderstand,
Causeth all our land
    So greatly to decay.

Meruell it is to heare
Of noble men, that were
Among vs many a yeare
    In the times past;

The which toke in hand
Prouifion fhold be fand
For to inhabit this land,
    And this was all their caft.

To bylde churches ftrong,
With folemne belles rong,
Deuine feruice fong,
    Mans life to amend :
Than was dubbed many a knight,
With all their powre and might
Holy Church and right
    Sworne to defende.

Than made they fuch ordynance,
That euerie man with reuerence
Vnder the law and obedience
    Their prince fhould obay ;
And while this people pure,
Their goodnes did endure,
So long, I you enfure,
    This land might not decay.

Than the king fet good price
By noble men and wyfe,
And after their deuife
    He did gouerne him felfe :
He wold not forfake
Their counfell to take :
They wold no ftatute make
    But for the common welth.

Than was he held in honor:
The king liued in great pleasure,
And among his people great treasure,
    For no thing wold they care.
Than were men both freshe and bolde,
And kept a noble householde:
The people had what they wolde;
    Few of them were bare.

Mery hartes were then to ryde
Thorough townes and cyties wide,
Replenished on euery syde
    With castels and towers hie;
But now are the captaynes gone,
There is not lefte the xth at home:
The goodly towers of lime and stone,
    A long on the ground they lye.

Castels now be not set by,
The cause is well knowne why:
Sithe they be downe, let them lye,
    They stop not my way.
They stood my fathers time before:
If they doe mine, I aske no more,
And so of them men kepe no store,
    For with cause they do decaye.

The people liue in variaunce
For lacke of perseueraunce:
Simple is their gouernaunce,
    And worse is their entent.

Euery man is now fayne
On other to complaine :
If this long remaine,
    Wee ſhall all repent.

The ſpiritualty their miſliuing,
To the temporalty enſample giuing,
And thus eithers worke reprouing,
    They lyue in bate and ſtrife.
The lay men ſay that prieſtes jet,
All fiſhe that commeth to net :
They ſpare nought they can get,
    Whether maide or wife.

Men ſay priors and abbotts bee
Great ingroſſers in this countrie :
They vſe bying and ſelling openlye :
    The Church hath the name.
They are not content with their poſſeſſion,
But add thereto by oppreſſion,
Still gaping for promotion,
    Vnto our landes great ſhame.

And in like wiſe the commynaltie
Apply them ſelues right conſtantlie
To learne crafte and ſubtiltie,
    Their neighbours to begyle :
The ſiſter will begyle the brother,
The childe will begyle the mother,
And thus none will truſt an other,
    If this world laſt a whyle.

Temporall lords be well nie gone :
Houfcholdes keepe they fewe or none,
Which caufeth many a poore man
    For to begge his bread.
If he fteale for his neceffity,
There is none other remedy,
But the law will very fhortly
    Hang him all faue the head.

And fome people, with great crueltie,
Vfe the law with extremitie,
The world is all without pitie :
    Of God they haue no drede.
In fuch pryde the world is brought,
By able men they fet right naught,
Which ere long wilbe forthought
    If of them they fhall haue nede.

The miforder of euerie cytie
Cawfeth great dearth and pouertie.
And alas! it is great pitie
    That rich men bee fo blynd :
Which for their pride and fulfome fare,
Will plucke their neighbours bare,
And thus the people punifhed are,
    And quickly brought behind.

A rich man without wifedom,
A wife man without difcretion,
A foole naturall for his promotion
    A ruler fhall become :

Then ſhall he maruelous ſtatutes try
Made by his great pollicy:
The rich be aduaunced thereby,
    And the poore be cleane vndone.

Now is made marchandiſe
Bying and ſelling benefice:
A lay man will therein enterpriſe
    That knoweth not the charge.
Craftes men now doe keepe a cure,
That with ſuch things were neuer in vre:
So he haue the tythe, ye may be ſure
    The paryſhe goeth at large.

Great men now take no heede
How ill ſo euer the commons ſpeede,
A poore man dare not ſpeake for drede,
    For nought can they recouer.
Some gratious man ſet to his hand,
That good prouiſion may be fand,
Or els farewell the welth of the land,
    Cleane vndone for euer!

Leaue the law, and vſe will:
To be perjured it ſhall not ſkill,
So that I may my bagges fill,
    And heyers to promote:
An other day then ſhall he
Be a ruler after me,
And ſo the poore comminaltie
    Be troden vnder fote.

Enuy wayith wondrous ſtrong,
The rich doth the poore wrong :
God of his mercy ſuffreth long
  The Deuill his workes to worke.
The townes go downe, the land decayes,
Of corn fields they make playne layes :
Great men maketh now a dayes
  A ſheepe cote of the church.

The places that we rightfully call
Places of Chriſtian buryall,
Of them they make an oxes ſtall :
  Theſe men be wonders wiſe.
Commons to cloſe and them to keepe,
While poore folke cry for bread & weepe :
Towns pulled downe to paſture ſheepe,
  This is the new guyſe.

Alyents alſo haue their way,
And Engliſhmen ſtill cleane decay :
The other halfe muſt needes play,
  This is the common wealth.
Other landes aduaunced bee,
And by and fell among us free,
And thus our owne commoditee
  Doth cleane vndoo our ſelfe.

Marchants all vſe ſubtilty :
The Church liueth viciouſly,
The commons are in pouerty :
  This land goeth to waſt.

The new guyse nowe a Dayes.

Marchaunt men trauell the countree,
Ploughmen dwell in the citie,
Which will deftroy us all fhortlie,
    As will be feene in haft.

To gather good great men be wyfe,
But yet they can no thing deuife,
That of their owne witt fhall arife
    For a common weale.
Their wittes on that they will not breake,
But if a man againft them fpeake,
Other remedy fhall he none feeke,
    But be carried ftraight to iaile.

    Imprinted by me R. Copland.

A prayer and also a thankesgiuing

vnto God, for his great mercy in giuing and preseruing our
Noble Queene Elizabeth to liue and reigne ouer
vs, to his honour and glory and our comfort
in Chrift Iefus: to be fung the xvii day
of November 1577.

Made by I. PIT, minifter.

*I exhort that fupplications, prayers and interceffions, and
giuing of thankes be made for Kings and for all that bee in
authoritie, that wee may lead a quiet and peaceable lyfe in all
godlynes and honeftie.* 1 Tim. 2, chap. 1, 2 verfes.

Sing this as the foure fcore and one Pfalme.

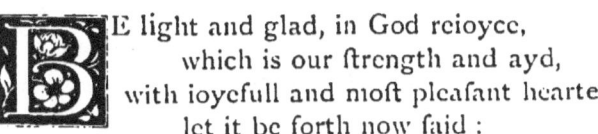E light and glad, in God reioyce,
    which is our ftrength and ayd,
    with ioyefull and moft pleafant heartes
      let it be forth now faid:

A prayer and also a thankesgiuing.

Thou art our Lord, thou art our King,
    thou art our only ſtay,
to thee will wee giue laud and praiſe,
    and further let vs ſay,

Wee praiſe thee, God, wee knowledge thee
    the only Lord to bee
for thy great mercy on vs ſhewde,
    as this day wee may ſee.
To thee wee cry, and alſo gyue
    moſt high thanks, laud and prayſe
for thy good giftes, which wee receiue
    both now and all our daies.

O holy, holy, holy Lord!
    ſhalbe our dayly ſong
for thy good giftes beſtowed on vs
    this ninetene yeres now long;
And for our Queen Elizabeth,
    which ſo long time hath been,
through thy good prouidence, O Lord!
    our good & gracious Queen.

The company of hygh and lowe
    doe prayſe thy holy name,
both yong and olde, both riche & poore
    with heart do euen the ſame,
Acknowledging thy maieſtie
    to be the only ſtay
through Chriſt our Lord & Sauiour,
    our light, our trueth, our way.

The holy ghoſt our comforter
      doth teach vs all in deed
how we ſhould walke in thy true feare,
      and call on thee in need,
For that our ſinnes moſt grieuous are,
      and do deſerue thine yre :
wee pray thee pardon vs ech one ;
      thy mercy wee require.

And graunt our Queene Elizabeth
      with vs long tyme to reigne,
this land to keepe ful long in peace,
      and goſpell to maineteine :
In true obedience of the ſame
      together we may lyue,
with long lyfe and moſt perfitte ioye,
      O Lord ! vnto her giue.

And giue vnto her councell grace,
      through working of this ſprite,
in goſpels lore and common wealthe
      to haue a great delight ;
The ſame to bring in perfite ſtate,
      and ſo the ſame to ſtay
againſt all wicked perverſe men,
      good Lord ! graunt this we pray.

Lord ! helpe thy feruants which do crye
      and cal to thee for ayd,
that enmies thence be put to flight,
      and wicked men diſmayd :

And let vs all moſt ioyfully
 with hearts tryumph and ſay,
thy name be bleſſed now, O Lord!
 for this moſt ioyfull day.

Wee magnifie thee euery one,
 and wil do while wee lyue,
for thy great mercy ſhewde on vs
 for this gift thou didſt giue;
Elizabeth our noble Queene,
 which as this day tooke place
in royall ſeat this Realme to guide,
 Lord, bleſſe and keepe her grace!

From foreine foes, O Lord! her keepe,
 and enemies at home,
from fained friends and trayterous hearts
 preſerue her, Lord, alone;
For thou only art her defence,
 in thee doth ſhee whole truſt:
ſaue and keepe her, O Lord, therefore
 for thy mercies moſt iuſt.

O Lord! our truſt and confidence
 wee do repoſe in thee,
for thou doeſt neuer ſayle them, Lord,
 that do put truſt in thee:
With faithfull hearts we do now pray
 that thou wilt ſo maintaine
our gracious Queen Elizabeth
 long ouer vs to raigne.

A prayer and alfo a thankesgiuing.

Then fhall wee fing with ioyfull hearts
    All glory be to thee
the Father, Sonne, and holy Ghoft
    which be in perfons three!
As it hath bene in all the time
    that hath bene heretofore,
as it is now, and fo fhalbe
    hence forth for euermore.
                  Amen.

1 Theffalonians the v Chap. 16, 17 and 18 verfes.

Reioyce euer. Praye continually. In all things giue thankes for this is the will of God in Chrift Iefus towards you.

                  FINIS.

Imprinted by Chriftopher Barkar.

Alowed by authoritie.

Englands Lamentation

For the late Treasons conspired against the Queenes
Maiestie by Frances Throgmorton: who was exe-
cuted at Tyborne, on the 10 day of July,
Anno 1584.

To the tune of Weepe, weepe.

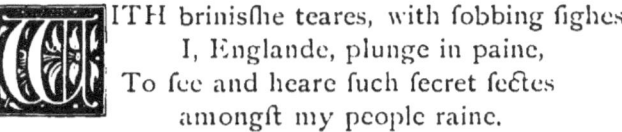ITH brinishe teares, with sobbing sighes,
I, Englande, plunge in paine,
To see and heare such secret sectes
amongst my people raine.

Now being in my golden prime
    where nectar sweete doth flowe,
And where Gods sacred worde is taught,
    eche Christians ioye to showe.
        Pray, pray, and praise the Lord, &c.

And where the Lord of Lords hath set,
    his handmaide pure and cleene,
Annoynting her my rightfull Prince,
    to raigne a royall Queene:
Indued with wisedome from above,
    and storde with knowledge great,
That flying Fame through all the world
    her praises doth repeate.
        Pray, pray, &c.

Who to the sacred worde doth stande
    with zeale and godly minde,
Maintaining truth, embracing faith,
    and to eche subject kinde.
Alas! why then, my people deare,
    what is the cause you swerue
Against the Lords annoynted, so
    your owne selfe willes to serue?
        Pray, pray, &c.

Haue you not peace and plentie store,
    which other realmes do want?
Haue you not worldly pleasures more,
    whereof there is no skant?
Haue I not fostered you with foode,
    which Nature yeelds not loth?

Englands lamentation.

Haue I not fed you dayntily
    with milke and hony both?
      Pray, pray, &c.

And haue not I a carefull Prince,
    the prop of all our stay,
Which loueth me, which cares for you,
    and prayes for vs eche day?
What is the cause such mischiefes then,
    among you doe remaine?
Truely the fulnes of the flesh,
    which you so much obtaine.
      Pray, pray, &c.

It makes me weepe with trickling teares,
    and wring my hands full colde,
To heare, to see, and thinke vpon
    the dangers manyfolde
My louing Prince and Queene is in,
    by meanes of Satans crew:
Which often doth conspire the death
    of her, my louer true.
      Pray, pray, &c.

How many mischeefes are deuised!
    how many wayes are wrought!
How many vilde conspiracies
    against her Grace are brought!
Yet God that rules in heauens aboue,
    lookes downe on earth below,
And dauntes them in their wickednesse,
    and his great power doth showe.

For when hir highnes doth not fee
    what dangers are at hande,
Then doth he fhewe by fecret meanes,
    thofe perils to withftande;
And will not let his chofen flocke
    to perifhe on the earth,
And doth her fecret foes confounde,
    by doome of fhamefull death.
        Pray, pray, &c.

As late was feene by Arden he,
    and Sommeruile alfo,
Who did pretende to kill my Queene,
    and worke her fubjects woe :
But God, who doth her ftill defende,
    her Grace he did preferue,
And wrought a fhame vnto them all,
    as they did beft deferue.
        Pray, pray, &c.

Throgmorton lately did confpire
    to ouerthrowe the State :
That ftrangers might inuade the realme
    vpon an euening late,
And lande in places where he knewe
    the realme was fomething weake ;
The fecret of which thing he did
    to forraigne Princes breake.
        Pray, pray, &c.

His dealing with the Queene of Scottes
    by letters too and fro,

Informed her and other states
    of all that he did knowe:
What frends in England they should find,
    what power they must neede,
Our Queene thereby for to displace:
    this was a treacherous deede.
        Pray, pray, &c.

He sought to dispossesse my Queene
    of dignitie and crowne,
And place a stranger on her throne,
    to tread her people downe.
Ireland and Scotland by aduise,
    the enemie should inuade;
Then into England bring a power,
    as he the plot had laide.
        Pray, pray, &c.

These were the treasons which he wrought
    my good Queene to displace;
To spoyle the state of all this realme,
    such was his want of grace:
But God, who doth protect me still,
    offended at the same,
Euen in his yong and tender yeeres,
    did cut him off with shame.
        Pray, pray, &c.

O thou, Throgmorton, wicked youth!
    why didst thou this despight?
Why did the feare of God and prince,
    depart so from thy sight?

No rebelles power shall her displace ;
   God will defende her still :
Her subiectes all will lose their liues,
   ere traytors haue their will.
      Pray, pray, &c.

And though he florisht for a time,
   in seeking his intent,
When to the pits brinke that he came,
   God did his worke preuent :
And did preserue in spight of him,
   his chosen vessell pure,
That she might florish still in peace
   my comfort to procure.
      Pray, pray, &c.

When as the seruants of the Lorde,
   I meane the Children three,
Were put into the fierie ouen,
   destroyed for to bee,
Then fierie flames did them no harme,
   they sung and prayed with ioye ;
And those which stood to worke their woe,
   the blases did destroye.
      Pray, pray, &c.

And when the children of the Lord
   King Pharao did pursue,
To drowne them in the foming floods,
   God was a captaine true :
The waues like walles stood on eche side,
   and they free passage founde,

Englands lamentation.

Whilſt Pharao with his mightie hoſte
    came after, and were drounde.
        Pray, pray, &c.

Euen ſo the Lord, by his great might,
    my comfort doth maintaine,
In keeping and preſeruing right
    my Prince from traitors traine :
And did preſerue her from the harmes
    Throgmorton did pretende ;
Who euen at Tyborne for his crimes
    did make a ſhamefull ende.
        Pray, pray, &c.

And though ſuch impes do worke her ſpight
    ten thouſande kinde of waies;
Yea, though the deuill him ſelfe do fight
    to ſpoyle her golden daies ;
Yet if the Lorde defende my wrong,
    their courage ſoone ſhall quaile :
So long as God ſtands on her ſide,
    what power can preuaile ?
        Pray, pray, &c.

Therefore, my louing people, heare,
    graunt England her requeſt :
Pray to the Lord, him ſerue with feare,
    and traitors hearts deteſt.
Embrace the truth, lay holde on faith,
    walke in the path of peace ;

Obey your Prince, maintaine her caufe,
    and Englands wealth encreafe.
        Pray, pray, &c.

And with new warning take new hearts,
    olde venomed minds deteft ;
Efchue all finne, encreafe good workes,
    that you in peace may reft.
From all olde cuftomes that are euill,
    put on the new man Chrift :
And newly change your former liues,
    and learne to pleafe the higheft.
        Pray, pray, &c.

FINIS.

W. M.

At London, imprinted by T H.

¶ An Epytaphe upon the Death of M. Rycharde Goodricke, Esquier.

---o---

YF euer Realme had caufe to rue
 The death and loffe of any one,
 Then hath this realme juft caufe and true
 This worthy dead man to bemone,
By whom fuche treafure theyr is lofte,
As fcant the lyke in Englandes cofte.

A heade where learned Pallas fate,
And fettled wyfdome dwelte lykewife,
And grounded fkyll for cōmon ftate
That with forecafte coulde well deuyfe :
 Where learnynge fyttes, with fkyll & wit,
 Suche one to rule who thynkes not fyt.

A tonge that prudently coulde faye
What myght be fayde, and that with fpede ;

A wyt that knewe no ftoppe nor ftaye
To gyue aduife in tyme of nede :
  A fytter matche there coulde not be
  Then tonge and wyll, thus to agree.

A hearte mofte earneft to mayntayne
Goddes trueth, and his vnfpotted lawe :
No hope of mede, no feare of payne,
From care of that coulde hym withdrawe.
  O bleffed realme, whofe rulers be
  So zelous in that thinge as he!

A man mofte redy to defende
A ryght, and here a poore mans caufe ;
No threatnynge foe, no fawnynge frende,
Coulde make hym do agaynfte the lawe.
  As lawes defende a trueth and ryght,
  So lawyers fhulde, withall theyr might.

Thus then the poore his helpe doth mys,
And Pallas lackes her learned knyght ;
The lawe doth lacke a lyght of his,
The realme hath lofte a worthy wyght ;
  And that whiche is the greateft gryefe,
  Goddes worde hath loft a membre chiefe.

And yet not loft, whom Chrift hath founde
And placed in heauen, I doubte it not.
Thus he that lackte his legges on grounde
Before vs all to heauen is got.
  To heauen, we fe, the neareft waye
  Is vertue then ; there is no naye.

    FINIS.   *R. M.*

31

The Cobler of Colchester.

A merry new Song, wherein is shewed the sorowfull cudgelling of the Cobler of Colchester by his Wife, for the eating of her Apple Pye.

To a pleasant new Tune called Trill lill.

 ALKING abroad, not long agoe,
    It was my chance to spye
A Coblers wife, with crabbed looke,
    How shee her strength did trie:
A cudgell great she had in hand,
    Both strong and tough withall,

The which about her husbands pate
    She broke in peeces fmall;
So that the man to crye began,
    With voice both loud and fhrill;
But banging about with courage ftout,
    She cryed, Haue with you, trill lill!

Good people, quoth the Cobler then,
    I pray you take the paine
To faue me from my angry wife,
    Or els I fhall be flaine.
The proudeft fcab in place, quoth fhe,
    May do it if he dare;
And he fhall beare a broken pate
    From hence, by Gis I fweare.
With that again fhe goes amaine
    to worke on him her will,
And euer fhe cryeth, as on him fhe flyeth,
    Haue with you, my hartes, trill lill!

Now, Cobler, quoth this cruell queane,
    Tell mee, and do not lye,
How thou doft like the eating of
    My owne fweete apple pye?
O wife! quoth hee, the worft to mee
    That euer I did taft:
I will be ware, if thou me fpare,
    How I do make fuch wafte.
To faue his life then fome come in,
    For feare fhe would him kill,
Where banging about with courage ftout,
    She cryde, My hartes, trill lill!

Now, fye for fhame! you are to blame
    Your husband thus to bang.
Tis better beare fome blowes, fhe faid,
    Than he hereafter hang:
A jewell he did breake and fpoile,
    Which I efteemed deare,
And I will not forgiue the fame,
    No, not this twenty yeare.
You need not blame, though I fhould lame
    The old knaue for this ill.
Then banging about with courage ftout,
    She cryed, My harts, trill lill!

Beleeue me, quoth the Cobler then,
    This thing is nothing fo:
For eating of her apple pye
    She hath wrought me this wo;
And tafting of a cuftard fmall,
    She for her felfe did keepe,
She hath mifus'd me, as you fee,
    And made me bleede & weepe.
Thus in defpight fhe takes delight
    To plague me at her will,
And euer fhe cryeth, as on me fhe flyeth,
    Haue with you, my harts, trill lill!

Gip with a murrain, knaue! fhe cryes,
    Muft your old chaps be fed
With cuftards and with apple pyes?
    A rope fhall ftretch your head.

I'll teache you take the browne rye loafe,
    and chaw the Essex cheese,
As fitter for your rotten teeth
    Then any one of these.
Then she began her owne good man
    to course him at her will;
And euer she cryeth, as on him she flyeth,
    Haue with you, my harts, trill lill!

And though, quoth she, indifferent well
    Thy carcas I did bumme,
Yet from thy carion greedy guts
    I'le fetch out euery crumme.
With that she did a feather take,
    And in his throate it thrust,
Till vp he cast the apple pye,
    The fruite as well as crust.
The dogs, quoth shee, shall eate it free,
    Ere it thy guts shall fill:
And euer she cryeth as on him she flyeth,
    Haue with you, my harts, trill lill!

Lo! here the spitefull nature plaine
    Wherewith she was possest,
For neuer was there any man
    Like this poore cobler drest:
Who made an oath, while he did liue,
    Such wisedome to apply,
He would take heede how he did eate
    His wife's owne apple pye,

The Cobler of Colchester. 35

Least with that wife he fell at strife,
    And felt her froward will,
Who euer cryeth, as on him she flyeth,
    Haue with you, my hartes, trill lill!

Imprinted at London by Andrew Wife, and are to be
sold at his shop in Paules Church-yard.

A proper new Ballad,

breefely declaring the Death and Execution of 14 moſt wicked Traitors, who ſuffered death in Lincolnes Inne feelde neere London: the 20 and 21 of September, 1586.

To the tune of Weep, weep.

REIOYCE in hart, good people all,
    ſing praiſe to God on hye
    Which hath preſerued vs by his power
    from traitors tiranny ;
Which now haue had their due deſarts,
    in London lately ſeen ;
And Ballard was the firſt that died
    for treaſon to our Queene.
      O praiſe the Lord with hart and minde,
      ſing praiſe with voices cleere,
      Sith traitcrous crue haue had their due,
      to quaile their parteners cheere.

Next Babington, that caitife vilde,
    was hanged for his hier:
His carcaffe likewife quartered,
    and hart caft in the fier.
Was euer feene fuch wicked troopes
    of traytors in this land,
Againft the pretious woord of truthe,
    and their good Queene to ftand?
    O praife, &c.

But heer beholde the rage of Rome,
    the fruits of Popifh plants;
Beholde and fee their wicked woorks,
    which all good meaning wants;
For Sauage alfo did receaue
    like death for his defert;
Which in that wicked enterprife
    fhould then haue doon his part.
    O praife, &c.

O curfed catifes, void of grace!
    will nothing ferue your turne,
But to beholde your cuntries wrack,
    in malice while you burne?
And Barnwell thou which went to view
    her grace in each degree,
And how her life might be difpatcht,
    thy death we all did fee.
    O praife, &c.

Confounding ſhame fall to their ſhare,
    and helliſh torments ſting,
That to the Lords annointed ſhall
    deuiſe ſo vile a thing!
O Techburne! what bewitched thee,
    to haue ſuch hate in ſtore,
Againſt our good and gratious Queene,
    that thou muſt dye therefore?
    O praiſe, &c.

What gaine for traitors can returne,
    if they their wish did win;
Or what preferment should they get
    by this their trecherous ſinne?
Though forraine power loue treaſon well,
    the traitors they diſpiſe,
And they the firſt that should ſuſtaine
    the ſmart of their deuiſe.
    O praiſe, &c.

What cauſe had Tilney, traitor ſtout,
    or Abbington likewiſe,
Againſt the Lords annointed thus
    ſuch miſcheef to deuiſe;
But that the Deuill inticed them
    ſuch wicked woorks to render;
For which theſe ſeuen did ſuffer death
    the twentith of September.
    O praiſe, &c.

Seauen more the next day following
    were drawen from the Tower,
Which were of their confederates,
    to dye that inftant hower :
The firft of them was Salsburie,
    and next to him was Dun,
Who did complaine moft earneftly
    of proud yong Babington.
        O praife, &c.

Both Lords and Knights of hye renowne
    he ment for to difplace ;
And likewife all our towers and townes,
    and cities for to race.
So likewife Iones did much complaine
    of his detefted pride,
And shewed how lewdly he did liue
    before the time he died.
        O praife, &c.

Then Charnock was the next in place
    to tafte of bitter death,
And praying vnto holy Saints,
    he left his vitall breath.
And in like maner Travers then
    did fuffer in that place,
And fearfully he left his life
    with croffing breaft and face.
        O praife, &c.

Then Gage was ftripped in his fhirt,
    who vp the lather went,
And fought for to excufe him felfe
    of treafons falce intent.
And Bellamie the laft of all
    did fuffer death that daye;
Vnto which end God bring all fuch
    as wifh our Queenes decay!
      O praife, &c.

O faulce and foule difloyall men!
    what perfon would fuppofe,
That clothes of veluet and of filke
    fhould hide fuch mortall foes?
Or who would think fuch hidden hate
    in men fo faire in fight,
But that the Deuill can turne him felfe
    into an angell bright?
      O praife, &c.

But, Soueraigne Queene, haue thou no care,
    for God which knoweth all,
Will ftill maintaine thy royall ftate,
    and giue thy foes a fall:
And for thy Grace thy fubiects all
    will make their praiers ftill,
That neuer traitor in the land
    may haue his wicked will.
      O praife, &c.

A proper new Ballad.

Whofe glorious daies in England heere
    the mighty God maintaine,
That long vnto thy fubiects ioye
    thy Grace may rule and raigne.
And, Lord! we pray for Chriftes fake,
    that all thy fecret foes
May come to naught which feeke thy life,
    and Englands lafting woes.
      O praife the Lord with hart and minde, &c.

The names of the 7 Traitors who were executed on Tuesday being the xx of September. 1586.	The names of the other vij which were executed on the next day after.
Iohn Ballard Preeft.	Thomas Salsbury.
Anthony Babington.	Henry Dun.
Iohn Sauage.	Edward Ihones.
Robert Barnwell.	Iohn Trauers.
Chodicus Techburne.	Iohn Charnock.
Charles Tilney.	Robert Gage.
Edward Abbington.	Harman Bellamy.

FINIS.   *T. D.*

Imprinted at London at the Long Shop
adioyning vnto Saint Mildreds
Churche in the Pultrie by
Edward Allde.

A fearefull and terrible Example

of Gods iuſte iudgement executed vpon a lewde Fellow,
who vſually accuſtomed to ſweare by
Gods Blood: which may be
A CAUEAT TO ALL THE WORLD
*That they blaſpheme not the name of their God
by Swearing.*

———o———

MORTALL men! which in this world
    for time haue your repaſt,
Approch the fearefulleſt thing to heare,
    and which hath happened laſt:
Yea, ſuch a thing as doth import
    the Lord our God on hye,

Through fwearing by his bleffed name,
    and that moft vfually.

Which ftraunge event whilft that I do
    perpend and to minde call,
My penne, in troth, is readie preft
    out of my hand to fall:
My hart alfo doth quaile in breft,
    my eyes diftill a pace,
The faulte and brinifh teares alfo
    do trickle downe my face.

But yet, good pen, hold on thy courfe,
    to write do thou not linne,
For I the truth to profecute
    hereof will now beginne.
There is a towne in Lincolnfhire,
    which Boothbie hath to name,
Juft three miles diftant from Grantham,
    a towne of ancient fame.

Wherein there dwells a gentleman,
    the truth for to decyde,
Who Frauncis Pennell called is:
    this may not be denyde.
It pleafed God this gentleman
    into his houfe to hire
A feruingman to attend on him,
    and borne in Worcefterfhire.

Which ſayd young man inclyned was
    vnto a thing not good,
As for to ſweare by Chriſt his fleſh,
    and by his precious blood :
It was his uſuall kinde of oath
    (O Sataniſt moſt vile)
Wherewith he did his liuing God
    pollute and eke defyle.

Meaning in iuſtice for to make
    this viper varlet he,
A terrour vnto all the world
    of ſwearing for to be.
Our Lord commaunded Death at him
    to ſhoote his fatall dart,
Who ſtraight, without protract of time,
    gorde him vnto the hart.

Now when that he the panges of death
    did feele and eke ſuſtaine,
Then he began, as you haue heard,
    Gods name for to blaſpheme ;
And neuer ceaſed for to ſweare
    by Ieſus Chriſt his blood,
Vntill his ſoule at the laſt gaſpe
    foorth of his body yood.

And in this cruell extaſie
    he paſſionate did lie
The ſpace of three or foure whole weekes,
    ſtill ſwearing bitterly.

Now when that he had languished
    the space that I haue sayde,
The people they perceiuing that
    of force he must be dead,

Caused the bell for to be tollde,
    that all for him might pray;
Beseeching God his soule to keepe
    against the dreadfull day.
But when that he had heard the bell
    knolling most drerilie,
He rushing vp said, by Gods blood
    this bell it tolles for me.

He had no sooner spoke these words
    which I haue shewd to you,
But that a pace his heart blood did
    foorth of his body flowe;
For why out of his fingers endes
    his blood did streame full fast,
So did it foorth at his toes endes,
    which made them all agaste.

And yet the Lord proceeded foorth
    this trayterous wight to scourge.
The blood gusht out, yea, at his wrists
    much like the foming surge;
So did it also at his nose
    runne foorth aboundantlie,
With other filthie excrements
    which man doth loathe to see.

Thus died he, committing
    his foule to Furies fell,
Which doe poffeffe th' infernall gulfe
    and laberinth of hell.
Than was his body ftraight interde,
    although in truth forlorne,
For whome it had beene better farre
    if he had not beene borne.

Whofe hart is now fo obdurate,
    that hearing of this thing
Will not permit out of the fame
    great flouds of teares to fpring;
Or whofe minde is fo fafcinate,
    or eke fo lullde on fleepe,
That for to heare hereof will not
    conftrained be to weepe?

And that for feare he fhould his God
    through fwearing thus offend,
And thereby purchafe to him felfe
    like dyre and rufull end.
O you! that fweare at euerie word,
    repleate with diuelrie,
For to abftaine from fwearing vile
    let this a caueat be.

For fure I am we neuer ought
    at any time to fweare,
Except the Chriftian magiftrate
    by lawe doo it require;

And if before him we doo fweare
    in truth and holineffe,
The Lord himfelfe acknowledgeth
    he thereby honourd is

And thus I end, befeeching God
    of his efpeciall grace,
That we all finfull fwearing may
    abandon in each place.
Elizabeth, our noble Queene,
    good Lord, preferue and fheeld,
That fhe thy chaft & faithfull fpowfe
    may ftill maintaine and build.

FINIS.

Philip Stubbes.

Imprinted at London for W. Wright, and
are to be fold at his fhop
in the Poultrie.

The Northern Lord.

IN FOUR PARTS.

To a pleasant new Tune.

———o———

NOBLE lord of high renowne
Two daughters had, the eldeſt browne;
The youngeſt beautifull and faire.
By chance a noble knight came there.

The father ſaid, Kind ſir, I haue
Two daughters, & which do you craue?
One that is beautifull, he cryed,
The noble knight he then replyed.

She's young, fhe's beautifull and gay,
And is not to be giuen away;
But, as jewels are bought and fold,
She fhall bring me her weight in gold.

The price, methinkes, you neede not grutch,
Since I will freely giue as much
With her owne fifter; if I can
Finde out fome other nobleman.

With that befpake the noble knight:
More welcome is the beauty bright
At that high rate, renowned lord,
Then the other with a vaft reward.

So then the bargain it was made;
But ere the money could be paide
He borrow'd it of a wealthy Iew,
The fum fo large. The writings drew,

That if he failde, or mifs'd his day,
So many ounces he fhould pay
Of his owne flefh, inftead of gold.
All was agreed; the fum was told.

So he return'd immediately
Vnto the lord, where he did buy
His daughter deare, of beautie rare,
And paide him downe the money there.

He bought her fo: it was well knowne
Vnto all men fhe was his owne.
By her a fon he did enioy,
A noble fweete and comely boy.

At length the time of pay drew neare,
Whenas the knight began to feare:
He dreaded much the cruell Jew,
Because the money then was dew.

His lady afkt him why he griev'd?
He faid, My jewell, I receiv'd
Such a huge fum, and of a Jew,
And with it I did purchafe you.

But now the day of payment's come,
I know not how to raife the fumme;
He'll haue my flefh, yea, weight for weight,
Which makes my griefe and forrow great.

Tush! neuer feare, the dame reply'd:
We'll crofs the raging ocean wide,
And fo fecure you from the fate.
To her requeft he yeelded ftrait.

PART II.

Then hauing paft the raging feas,
They trauail'd on, till by degrees
Vnto the German court they came;
The knight, his fonne, and comely dame.

The Northern Lord.

Vnto the emperor he told
His story of the summe of gold
That he had borrowd of a Iew,
And that for feare of death he flew.

The emperor he did erect
A court for them; and shewd respect
Vnto his guests, because they came
From Britain, that blest land of fame.

As here he liued in delight,
A Dutch lord told our English knight,
That he a ton of gold would lay
He could enioy his lady gay.

This Lord from her, then, was to bring
A rich and costly diamond ring,
That was to proue and testifie
How he did with his lady lye.

He tried, but neuer could obtaine
Her fauour, but with high disdaine
She did abhor his base intent;
So to her chambermaid he went,

And told her, if she would but steale
Her lady's ring, and so conceale
The same, and bring it to him strait,
She should enioy his whole estate.

In hopes of such a great reward
The ring she stole; and the Dutch lord

Did take it to the Englifh knight,
Who almoft fwounded at the fight.

Home goeth he to his lady ftrait :
Meeting her at the pallace gate,
He flung her headlong in the moate,
And left her there to finke or floate.

Soone afterward, in armour greene,
She like a warlike wight was feene;
And in moft gallant feemely fort
She rode vnto the emperors court.

Now, when the emperor behild
Her graue deportment, he was fill'd
With admiration at the fight,
Who call'd her felfe an Englifh knight.

The emperor did then reply :
An Englifh knight's condemn'd to dye
For drowning his falfe lady gay.
Quoth fhe, I'le free him, if I may.

PART III.

She to the emperor did ride,
And faid, Now let the caufe be tryde
Once more; for Iue refolu'd to faue
This noble gallant from the graue.

It was decreed, the court fhould fet.
The Dutch lord came, feeming to fret
About the ring; as if in feare
The truth would make his fhame appeare.

And fo it chanc'd; for foone they call
The maid, who on her knees did fall
Before the iudge, and did defcry
The Dutch lord's fhamefull treachery.

The court declared it to be fo:
The lady too, for ought we know,
May be aliue; therefore we ftay
The fentence till another day.

Now the Dutch lord gaue him the ton
Of gold, that he had iuftly wonne;
Which hauing done with fhame and griefe,
The Englifh lord had fome reliefe.

The Dutch lord, to reuenge the fpight
Upon our noble English knight,
Did fend a letter out of hand,
And gaue the Jew to underftand,

How he was in the German court:
Therefore, vpon this good report,
The Jew he croft the ocean wide,
Intent on being satisfied.

Soone as he fixt his greedy eies
Vpon the knight, in wrath he cries,

Your hand and feale I haue; behold!
Your flefh Ile haue inftead of gold.

Then faid the noble knight in greene:
Sir, may not the deed be feene?
Behold it here! replyed the Jew,
But I refolue to haue my due.

Lo! then the knight began to reade.
At laft he faid: I find in deede
Nothing but flesh you are to haue.
Anfwerd the Jew, That's all I craue.

The poore diftreffed knight was broght:
The bloody-minded Jew he thought
That day to be reuengde on him,
And cut his flefh from euery limb.

The knight in greene faid to the Iew.
Theres nothing els but flefh your due:
Then, fee no drop of blood you fhed,
For if you do, you lofe your head.

Now take your due with all my hart;
But with his blood we will not part.
With that the Iew foone went his way,
Nor had another word to fay.

PART IV.

No sooner were these troubles past
But the wifes father came in haft,
Determin'd for to haue his life
For drowning his beloued wife.

Ouer the seas her father brought
Many braue horses: one was bought
By the disguised knight in greene,
Which was the best that ere was seene.

They brought her lord from prison then,
Guarded by many armed men,
Vnto the place where he must dye;
And the greene knight was standing by.

Then from her side her sword she drew,
And ran her gelding through and through.
Her father askt, Why dost thou so?
I may; it is mine owne, you know.

You sold your gelding, 'tis well knowne;
I bought it, making it mine owne,
And may doe what I please with it.
So then to her he did submit.

Here is a man arraign'd and cast,
And brought to suffer death at last,
Because your daughter deare he slue;
But if he did, concerns it you?

You had your money, when you fold
Your daughter for her weight in gold :
Wherefore he might, as I haue fhowne,
Do what him pleafed with his owne.

Then, hauing chang'd her armour greene,
And dreft her felfe like to a queene,
Her father and her husband ftrait
Both knew her ; and their ioy was great.

Soone did they carry this report
Vnto the famous German court,
How the renowned English knight
Had found at length his lady bright.

The emperor and his lords of fame
With cheerfull harts did then proclaim
An vniuerfall ioy, to fee
This lady's life and libertie.

FINIS.

A warning to all false Traitors

BY EXAMPLE OF 14.

Wherof vi. were executed in diuers places neere about London, and 2 neere Braintford, the 28. day of Auguſt, 1588.

Alſo at Tyborne were executed the 30 *day vj. namely* 5 *Men and one Woman. To the tune of Greenſleeues.*

———o———

YOU traitors all that doo deuiſe
    To hurt our Queene in trecherous wiſe,
    And in your hartes doo ſtill ſurmize
        which way to hurt our England,
Conſider what the ende will be
Of traitors all in their degree,
Hanging is ſtill their deſtenye,
    that trouble the peace of England.

I

Will not examples make you true,
But you will ſtill the ſteppes enſue
Of the vngodly Romiſh crue
    that trouble the peace of England?
Remember Felton, long agoe,
And Campion that was hang'd alſo,
With a number great of traitors moe,
    that troubled the peace of England.

Then Parrie, and Throckmorton eke,
Of traiterous drifts were not to feeke,
And diuers other haue doone the like
    to trouble the peace of England:
And Babbington, with his wicked traine,
Continually did beate their braine
Which way and how they might obtaine
    to trouble the peace of England.

But God, we ſee, hath ſtill made knowne
Their wicked meaninges euery one,
And death hath made their harts to grone,
    that troubled the peace of England:
Yet will not theſe examples good
Once ſtay theſe traitors madding mood,
But ſtill they feeke to ſuck the blood,
    of our gratious Queene of England.

As late neer London there was ſeene
Two traitors hang'd on Myle-end greene,
Which did take part againſt our Queene,
    to trouble her realme of England:

The firft a preeft, his name was Deane,
The next was Weblin, who did meane
To helpe the Spaniards for to gleane
    the fruites of the realme of England.

The next in Finsberrie feeld their died
A preeft that was a traitor tryed,
His name was Gunter, who denied
    to helpe the good Queene of England :
But he would, for the Spaniards fake,
Prouide inuafion for to make,
And gainft our Queene their partes to take
    to trouble the peace of England.

There died in Lincolnes feelde also
Moorton, a cruell traitor, too,
He being a preeft, with other moe,
    did come to trouble our England :
And in that place there died with him
One Moore, that was a traitor grim,
Who would haue ventured life and lim
    to hurt the good Queene of England.

There died eke at Clarkenwell
A preeft, that was a traitor fell,
His name was Acton, trueth to tell,
    that troubled the peace of England;
For why, he fought for to maintaine
The Pope, and eke the Spanish traine,
And did our gratious Queene difdaine,
    with all that loue her in England.

Then Felton yong, who did upholde
The Pope, as did his father olde :
His falſe hart he to treaſon folde,
    to trouble the peace of England.
To Braintford he was had to dye,
Whereas he ſtoutly did deny
To helpe our Queene and her cuntrye,
    but fought the decay of England.

And in like manner Clarkſon, he
To Braintford went for company,
Where both were hanged vpon a tree
    as enemies to our England :
Both preeſts they were, of Romiſh rout,
Who ſubtilly did goe about
But yet for them it was no boot,
    to hurt the good realme of England.

At Tyborne dyed, the thirteth day,
Flewett and Shelley, trueth to ſay,
And Leigh, a preeſt, who did denay
    to aide the good Queene of England :
Martin and Rooche, that preſent died
At Tyborne, being traitors tryed ;
For, like the reſt, they had denide
    to aide the good Queene of England.

One Margeret Ward there died that daye,
For from Bridewell ſhe did conuay
A traiterous preeſt with ropes away,
    that fought to trouble our England :

This wicked woman, voide of grace,
Would not repent in any case,
But defperatly even at that place,
 she died as a foe to England.

When law had paffed upon them fo,
They fhould be hang'd and quartered too,
Our Queene tooke mercy on them tho,
 which fought her decay in England,
And pardoned them their greateft paine;
Yet all her pitie was in vaine,
For to afke mercy they did difdaine
 of the gratious Queene of England.

But God, we fee, dooth ftill defend
Our gratious Queene unto the end,
Gainft traitors that doe ill pretend
 to her and her realme of England.
God graunt that we may thankfull be
Vnto his glorious Maieftie,
That fo defendes the foueraignty
 of the vertuous Queene of England.

The names of the 8. Traytors executed on the
eight and twentith of Auguft.

William Deane and Henry Webley, executed at Myle-end.

William Gunter, executed at Fins-burye.

Robert Moorton and Hugh Moore, executed in Lincolns Inne feelde.

Thomas Acton, executed at Clarkenwell.

Thomas Felton and Iames Clarkſon, executed neere Braintford.

The names of them that were executed the
30 of Auguſt.

Richard Flewett, Edward Shelley, Richard Leigh, Richard Martin and Iohn Rooche, executed at Tyborne.

Alſo at the ſame time one Margaret Ward for letting a Seminarye Prieſte out of Bridewell.

FINIS.

Imprinted at London by Edward Allde
at the long ſhop near
vnto S. Mildreds
Church.

The Lamentation of Mr. Pages Wife

Of Plimouth, who, being forc'd to wed him, confented to his
Murder, for the loue of G. Strangwidge: for
which they fuffered at Barnftable
in Devonfhire.

The Tune is Fortune my Foe, &c.

———o———

NHAPPY fhe whom Fortune hath forlorne,
Defpis'd of grace that profferd grace did
 fcorne,
My lawleffe loue hath luckleffe wrought my
 woe,
My difcontent content did ouerthrowe.

The lamentation of Mr. Pages wife.

My lothed life to late I doe lament,
My wofull deedes in heart I doe repent:
A wife I was that wilfull went awry,
And for that fault am here preparde to dye.

In blooming yeares my Father's greedy minde,
Against my will, a match for me did finde:
Great wealth there was, yea, gold and siluer store,
But yet my heart had chosen one before.

Mine eies dislikt my fathers liking quite,
My hart did loth my parents fond delight:
My childish minde and fancie told to mee,
That with his age my youth could not agree.

On knees I prayde they would not me constraine;
With teares I cryde their purpose to refraine;
With sighes and sobbes I did them often moue,
I might not wed whereas I could not loue.

But all in vaine my speeches still I spent:
My mothers will my wishes did preuent.
Though wealthy Page possest the outward part,
George Strangwidge still was lodged in my hart.

I wedded was, and wrapped all in woe;
Great discontent within my hart did growe:
I loathd to liue, yet liude in deadly strife,
Because perforce I was made Pages wife.

My closen eies could not his sight abide;
My tender youth did lothe his aged side:

The lamentation of Mr. Pages wife.

Scant could I taste the meate whereon he fed;
My legges did lothe to lodge within his bed.

Cause knew I none I should dispise him so,
That such disdaine within my hart should growe,
Saue onely this, that fancie did me moue,
And told me still, George Strangwidge was my loue.

Lo! heere began my downfall and decay.
In minde I musde to make him strait away:
I that became his discontented wife,
Contented was he should be rid of life.

Methinkes the heauens crie uengeance for my fact,
Methinkes the world condemns my monstrous act,
Methinkes within my conscience tells me true,
That for that deede hell fier is my due.

My pensiue soule doth sorrow for my sinne,
For which offence my soule doth bleed within;
But mercy, Lord! for mercy still I crye:
Saue thou my soule, and let my bodie dye.

Well could I wish that Page enioyde his life,
So that he had some other to his wife:
But neuer could I wish, of low or hie,
A longer life then see sweete Strangwidge die.

O woe is me! that had no greater grace
To stay till he had runne out Natures race.
My deedes I rue, but more I doe repent
That to the same my Strangwidge gaue consent.

K

You parents fond, that greedy-minded bee,
And feeke to graffe vpon the golden tree,
Confider well and rightfull iudges bee,
And giue your doome twixt parents loue and mee.

I was their childe, and bound for to obey,
Yet not to loue where I no loue could laye.
I married was to muck and endleffe ftrife;
But faith before had made me Strangwidge wife.

O wretched world! who cankerd ruft doth blind,
And curfed men who beare a greedy minde;
And hapleffe I, whom parents did force fo
To end my dayes in forrow, fhame, and wo.

You Denfhire dames, and courteous Cornwall knights,
That here are come to vifit wofull wights,
Regard my griefe, and marke my wofull end,
But to your children be a better frend.

And thou, my dear, that for my fault muft dye,
Be not affraide the fting of death to trye:
Like as we liude and loude together true,
So both at once we'le bid the world adue.

Ulalia, thy friend, doth take her laft farewell,
Whofe foule with thee in heauen fhall euer dwell.
Sweet Sauiour Chrift! do thou my foule receiue:
The world I doe with all my heart forgiue.

And parents now, whofe greedy mindes doe fhow
Your harts defire, and inward heauie woe,

Mourn you no more, for now my heart doth tell,
Ere day be done my foule fhalbe full well.

And Plimouth proude, I bid thee now farewell.
Take heede, you wiues, let not your hands rebel;
And farewell, life, wherein fuch forrow fhowes,
And welcome, death, that doth my corps inclofe.

And now, fweete Lord! forgiue me my mifdeedes.
Repentance cryes for foule that inward bleedes:
My foule and bodie I commend to thee,
That with thy bloud from death redeemed mee.

Lord! bleffe our Queene with long and happy life,
And fend true peace betwixt eche man and wife;
And giue all parents wifedome to forefee,
The match is marrde where mindes doe not agree.

T. D.

London.   Printed by Thomas Scarlet.   1591.

The Lamentation of George Strangwidge,

Who for the confenting to the death of Mr. Page of
Plymouth, fuffered death at Barnftable.

To the tune of Fortune.

———o———

HE man that fighs and forowes for his fin,
The corps which care and wo hath wrapped in,
In dolefull fort records his fwan-like fong,
That waits for death, and loths to liue fo long.

The lamentation of George Strangwidge.

O Glanfield! caufe of my committed crime,
So wed to wealth as birds in bufh of lime,
What caufe hadft thou to beare fuch wicked fpight
Againft my loue, and eke my harts delight.

I would to God thy wifedome had beene more,
Or that I had not entred at thy doore,
Or that thou hadft a kinder father beene
Unto thy child, whofe yeares are yet but greene.

The match vnmeete which thou alone didft make,
When aged Page thy daughter home did take,
Well maift thou rue with teares that cannot drie,
Which is the caufe that foure of vs muft dye.

Ulalia, more bright then fummers funne,
Whofe beauty had my loue for euer wonne,
My foule more fobs to thinke of thy difgrace,
Then to behold my owne vntimely race.

The deede late done in hart I doe repent,
But that I lou'de I cannot it relent:
Thy feemly fight was euer fweete to me.
Would God my death could thy excufer be!

It was for me, alas! thou didft the fame,
On me by right they ought to laye the blame:
My worthleffe loue hath brought thy life in fcorne.
Now, wo is me that euer I was borne!

Farewell, my loue, whofe loyall hart was feene:
Would God thou hadft not halfe fo conftant beene!

The lamentation of George Strangwidge.

Farewell, my loue, the pride of Plymouth towne;
Farewell the flowre, whofe beauty is cut downe.

For twentie yeares great was the coft, I knowe,
Thine vnkind father did on thee beftow;
Yet afterward fo fowre did fortune lowre,
He loft his ioy, his childe, within an howre.

My wrong and wo to God I doe commit.
Who was the caufe of matching them unfit?
And yet my guilt I can not fo excufe,
We gaue confent his life for to abufe.

Wretch that I am, that my confent did giue!
Had I denyde, Ulalia ftill fhould liue.
Blind fancy faide, this fute doe not deny;
Liue thou in bliffe, or els in forow dye.

O Lord! forgiue this cruell deede of mine:
Vpon my foule let beames of mercy fhine.
In iuftice, Lord, doe thou not uengeance take:
Forgiue us both for Jefus Chrift his fake.

FINIS.

Imprinted at London by E. Allde.

The Complaint of Walltia,

For causing of her Husband to be murdered for the love of Strangwidge, who were executed together.

To the tune of Fortune my foe.

———o———

F ever wo did touch a womans hart,
Or griefe did gaul for sin the outward part,
My conscience, then, and heauy hart within
Can witnes well the sorrow for my sinne.

The complaint of Ulallia.

When yeares were young, my father forſt me wed
Againſt my will, where fancie was not fed :
I was content his pleaſure to obay,
Although my hart was linckt another way.

Great were the guifts they profferd in my fight,
With wealth they thought to win me to delight ;
But gold nor guifts could not my minde remoue,
And I was linckt whereas I could not loue.

Methought his ſight was lothſome to mine eie ;
My hart did grudge againſt him inwardly.
This diſcontent did cauſe my deadlie ſtrife,
And with this wealth did cauſe a grieuous life.

My conſtant loue was on yong Strangwidge ſet,
And wo to him that did our welfare let :
His loue ſo deepe a hold in me did take,
I would haue gone a begging for his ſake.

Wronged he was through fond deſire of gaine,
Wronged he was ene through my parents plaine.
If faith and troth a perfect pledge might bee,
I had beene wife vnto no man but hee.

Eternall God ! forgiue my fathers deede,
And graunt all maidens may take better heede.
If I had beene but conſtant to my frend,
I had not matcht to make ſo bad an end.

But wanting grace, I fought my owne decay,
And was the caufe to make my friend away;
And he on whom my earthlie ioyes did lie,
Through my amifs a fhamefull death muft dye.

Farewell, fweete George, always my louing frend,
Needs muft I laud and loue thee to the end;
And albeit that Page poffeft thy due,
In fight of God thou waft my husband true.

My watery eyes vnto the heauens I bend,
Crauing of Chrift his mercie to extend.
My bloudy deede to me, O Lord! forgiue,
And let my foule within thy kingdome liue.

Farewell, falfe world, and friends that fickle be;
All wiues farewell; example take by mee:
Let not the Deuill to murder you infpire,
Seeke to efcape fuch foule and filthie mire.

And now, O Chrift! to thee I yeeld my breath,
Strengthen my faith in bitter pangues of death;
Forgiue my faults and folly of my times,
And with thy bloud wafh thou away my crimes.

FINIS.

Printed by I. R. for Edward White.

The Weauers Song

IN THE PRAISE OF LOUE AND FRIENDSHIP.

To the tune of Apelles.

HEN Hercules did vfe to fpin,
    And Pallas wrought vpon the loome,
Our trade to flourifh did begin,
    While Confcience went not felling broome:
Then loue and friendfhip did agree
    To keepe the bands of amitie.   I.

The Weauers Song.

When princes fons kept fheepe in field,
   And queenes made cates of wheaten flowre,
Then men to lucre did not yeeld,
   Which brought good cheere in euery bowre.
Then loue and friendfhip did agree, &c.

But when the gyants huge and hie
   Did fight with fpeares like weauers beames,
Then they in yron beds did lie,
   And brought poore men to hard extreames :
Yet loue and friendfhip did agree, &c.

Then Dauid tooke his fling and ftone,
   Not fearing great Goliaths ftrength ;
He pearc't his braine and broke the bone,
   Though he was fifty foote in length.
For loue and friendfhip did agree, &c.

The whiles the Greekes befieged Troy
   Penelope apace did fpin,
And weauers wrought with mickle ioy,
   Though gains were flow in comming in.
For loue and friendfhip did agree, &c.

Had Helen then fat carding wooll,
   Whofe beauteous face did breede the ftrife,
Shee had not been Sir Paris trull,
   Nor caus'd fo many lofe their life ;
Yet we by loue did ftill agree, &c.

Or had King Pryams wanton fonne
    Been making quills with fweete content,
He had not all his friends vndone,
    When he to Greece a gadding went.
For loue and friendfhip did agree, &c.

The cedar trees indure more ftormes
    Then little fhrubs that fprout not hie:
The weauer liues more voide of harmes
    Then princes of great dignitie.
While loue and friendfhip doe agree, &c.

The fhepheard fitting in the field
    Doth tune his pipe with hearts delight:
When princes watch with fpeare and fhield,
    The poore man foundly fleeps at night.
While loue and friendfhip doe agree, &c.

Yet this by proofe is dayly tride,
    For Gods good gifts we are ingrate,
And no man through the world fo wide
    Liues well contented with his ftate.
No loue or friendfhip we can fee
    To hold the bands of amitie.

London, Printed for E. White.

Agincourt,

OR THE ENGLISH BOWMANS GLORY.

To a pleafant new Tune.

———o———

GINCOURT, Agincourt!
Know ye not Agincourt,
Where Englifh flue and hurt
   All their French foemen?
With their pikes and bills brown,
How the French were beat downe,
   Shot by our Bowmen!

Agincourt, Agincourt!
Know ye not Agincourt,
Neuer to be forgot,
   Or known to no men?
Where Englifh cloth-yard arrows
Kill'd the French, like tame fparrows,
   Slaine by our Bowmen.

Agincourt, Agincourt!
Know ye not Agincourt,
Where we won field and fort,
   French fled like wo-men?
By land, and eke by water,
Neuer was feene fuch flaughter,
   Made by our Bowmen.

Agincourt, Agincourt!
Know ye not Agincourt?

Englifh of euery fort,
    High men and low men,
Fought that day wondrous well, as
All our old ftories tell us,
    Thankes to our Bowmen!

Agincourt, Agincourt!
Know ye not Agincourt?
Either tale or report
    Quickly will fhow men
What can be done by courage;
Men without food or forage,
    Still lufty Bowmen.

Agincourt, Agincourt!
Know ye not Agincourt?
Where fuch a fight was fought,
    As, when they grow men,
Our boys fhall imitate,
Nor neede we long to waite;
    They'll be good Bowmen.

Agincourt, Agincourt!
Know ye not Agincourt?
Where our fift Harry taught
    Frenchmen to know men;
And when the day was done
Thoufands there fell to one
    Good Englifh Bowman.

Agincourt, Agincourt!
Huzza for Agincourt!

When that day is forgot
   There will be no men :
It was a day of glory,
And till our heads are hoary
   Praife we our Bowmen.

Agincourt, Agincourt!
Know ye not Agincourt?
When our beft hopes were nought,
   Tenfold our foemen,
Harry led his men to battle,
Slue the French like fheep and cattle,
   Huzza! our Bowmen.

Agincourt, Agincourt!
Know ye not Agincourt?
O, it was noble fport!
   Then did we owe men:
Men who a victory won us
Gainft any odds among us:
   Such were our Bowmen.

Agincourt, Agincourt!
Know ye not Agincourt?
Deare was the victory bought
   By fifty yeomen.
Afk any English wench,
They were worth all the French:
   Rare English Women!

FINIS.

Printed for Henry Harper in Smithfield.

A ioyfull new Ballad,

Declaring the happie obtaining of the great Galeazzo, wherein Don Pedro de Valdez was the Chiefe, through the mightie Power and Prouidence of God; being a speciall token of his gracious and fatherly goodnesse towards vs: to the great encouragement of all those that willingly fight in defence of his Gospell, and our good Queene of England.

———o———

NOBLE England!
    fall downe vpon thy knee,
And prayse thy God with thankfull hart
    which still maintaineth thee.

The forraine forces
 that feeke thy vtter fpoyle
Shall then through his efpeciall grace
 be brought to fhamefull foyle.

With mighty power
 they came vpon our coaft:
To ouer runne our countrie quite,
 they made their brag and boaft.
In ftrength of men
 they fet their onely ftay,
But we vpon the Lord our God
 will put our truft alway.

Great is their number
 of fhippes vpon the fea,
And their prouifion wonderfull,
 but, Lord! thou art our ftay:
Their armed fouldiers
 are many by account,
Their aiders eke in this attempt
 doe fundrie wayes furmount.

The Pope of Rome,
 with many bleffed graines,
To fanctify their bad pretence
 beftowde both coft and paines:
But, little Ifland,
 be not difmayde at all;
The Lord, no doubt, is on our fide,
 which foone will worke their fall.

A ioyfull new Ballad.

In happie hower
    our foes we did difcry,
All vnder faile with gallant winde
    as they came paffing by.
Which fodaine tidings
    to Plymouth being brought,
Full foone our Lord high Admirall
    for to purfue them fought.

And to his men
    courageoufly he faide,
Now for the Lord, and our good Queene
    to fight be not afraide.
Regard our caufe,
    and play your partes like men.
The Lord, no doubt, will profper vs
    in all our actions then.

This great Galeazzo
    which was fo huge and high,
That like a bulwarke on the fea
    did feeme to each mans eie:
There was it taken
    vnto our great reliefe,
And diuers nobles, in which traine
    Don Pedro was the chiefe.

Strong was fhe ftuft
    with cannon great and fmall,
And other inftruments of warre,
    which we obtained all:

A certaine figne
  of good fucceffe, we truft,
That God will ouer throw the reft,
  as he hath done the firft.

Then did our nauie
  purfue the reft amaine,
With roaring noife of cannons great
  till they neere Callis came.
With manly courage
  they followed them fo faft,
An other mighty Galleon
  they made to yeeld at laft.

And in diftreffe,
  for fafegard of their liues,
A flag of truce they did hang out
  with many mournfull cries.
Which when our men
  did perfectly efpye,
Some little barkes they fent to her
  to board her prefently.

But thefe falfe Spanyards,
  efteeming them but weake,
When they within their danger came,
  their mallice foorth did breake.
With charged cannons
  they layde about them then,
For to deftroy thofe proper barkes,
  and all their valiant men.

Which when our men
　　perceiued fo to bee,
Like lions fierce they forward went
　　to quite this iniurie;
And boarding them
　　with ftrong and mightie hand,
They killd the men vntill the arke
　　did finke in Callice fand.

The chiefeft captaine
　　of this Galleon fo hye,
Don Hugo de Moncaldo he
　　in this fame fight did dye:
Who was the generall
　　of all the Galleons great,
But through his braines with powders force
　　a bullet ftrong did beat.

And many more
　　by fword did lofe their breath,
And many more within the fea
　　did fwimme and tooke their death.
There might you fee
　　the falt and foming floud
Dyed and ftaind like fkarlet red,
　　with ftore of Spanifh bloud.

This mightie veffell
　　was three fcore yards in length,
Moft wonderfull to each mans eie
　　for making and for ftrength:

In her was placed
    an hundred cannons great,
And mightily prouided eke
    with bread, corne, wine and meat.

There was of oares
    two hundered, I weene,
Three fcore foote and twelue in length
    well meafured to be feene:
And yet fubdued
    with many other more,
And not a fhip of ours loft:
    the Lord be thankt therefore!

Our pleafant countrie,
    fo fruitfull and fo faire,
They doe intend by deadly warre
    to make both poore and bare:
Our townes and citties
    to racke and facke likewife,
To kill and murther man and wife
    as malice doth auise.

And to deflower
    our virgins in our fight,
And in the cradle cruelly
    the tender babe to fmite:
Gods holy truth
    they meane for to caft downe,
And to depriue our noble Queene
    both of her life and crowne.

Our wealth and riches,
  which we enioyed long,
They doe appoint their pray and fpoyle
  by crueltie and wrong.
To fet our houfes
  a fire ore our heads,
And curfedly to cut our throats,
  as we lie in our beds.

Our childrens braines
  to dafh againft the ground,
And from the earth our memorie
  for euer to confound :
To change our ioy
  to griefe and mourning fad,
And neuer more to fee the dayes
  of pleafure we have had.

But God almightie
  be bleffed euer more,
Who doth encourage Englifhmen
  to driue them from our fhore ;
With roaring cannons
  their haftie fteps to ftay,
And with the force of thundring fhot
  to make them flie away.

Who made account
  before this time of daye,
Againft the walls of faire London
  their banners to difplay :

But their intent
> the Lord will bring to nought,
If faithfully we call and pray
> for fuccour, as we ought.

And you, deare brethren,
> which beareth armes this day
For fafeguard of your natiue foyle,
> marke well what I fhall fay :
Regarde well your duties,
> thinke on your countries good,
And feare not in defence thereof
> to fpend your deareft blood.

Our gratious Queene
> doth greete you euery our,
And faith fhe will amongft you be
> in every bitter ftoure ;
Defiring you
> true Englifh harts to beare
To God and her, and to the land
> wherein you nurfed were.

Lord God almightie
> which hath the harts in hand
Of every perfon to difpose,
> defend this Englifh land !
Bleffe thou our Soueraigne
> with long and happie life,
Indue her Councell with thy grace,
> and end this mortall ftrife.

Giue to the rest
    of Commons more or lesse,
Louing harts, obedient mindes,
    and perfect faithfulnesse,
That they and we,
    and all with one accord,
On Sion Hill may sing the prayse
    Of our all mightie Lord.

Imprinted at London by R. I.

The Good Shepeheard.

ALONG the verdant fields all richly dide
    With Natures paintments, and with Floras pride;
Whose goodly bounds are liuely chrystall streames,
Begirt with bowres to keepe backe Phœbus beames:

Euen when the quenchleffe torch, the Worlds great eie,
Aduanc't his rayes athwartly from the fkie,
And by his power and heauenly influence
Reuiude the feeds of Springs decaied effence:

Then manie flockes vnite in peace and loue,
Not feeking ought but naturall behoue,
Paft quietly, vnchargde with other care,
Saue of the feede within that pafture faire.

Thefe flockes a fhepheard had of power & fkill,
To fold and feede and faue them from all ill;
By whofe aduife they liude, whofe wholfome voyce
They heard, and feard with loue, and did reioyce

Therein with melodie of fong, and praife,
And daunce to magnifie his name alwaies.
He is their guide, they are his flocke and fold,
Nor will they bee by anie elfe controlld;

Well knowing that whom he takes care to feede,
He will preferue and faue in time of neede.
Thus liude this holy flocke at harts content,
Till cruell beafts, all fet on rauifhment,

Broke off their peace, and ran vpon with rage
Themfelues, their yong, and all their heritage,
Slitting their throates, deuouring lambes and all,
And diffipating them that fcapt the thrall.

Then did this iolly feaft to faft transforme,
(So afkt the fury of that ragefull ftorme)

Their ioyfull fong was turnd to mournfull cries,
And all their gladneffe chang'd to welladaies.

Whereat heauen grieuing clad it felfe in blacke,
And earth in vproare triumph'd at their wracke.
What profits then the fheepehooke of their guide,
Or that he lies vpon a beacons fide,

With watchfull eies to circumfcribe their traine,
And hath no more regard vnto the paine,
To faue them from the daunger imminent,
Say fome, as are fo often incident?

Tis not for that his arme wants ftrength to breake
All proud attempts that men of might doe make;
Or that he will abandon vnto death
His owne, deare bought with the exchange of breath.

Nor muft we thinke that though they dye they perifh:
Death dyes in them, and they in death reflourifh,
And this lifes loffe a better life renues
Which after death eternally enfues.

Though then their paffions neuer feeme fo great,
Yet neuer comfort wants to fwage their heate:
Though ftrength of torments be extreame in durance,
Yet are they quencht by hope and faithes affurance.

For thankfull hope, if God be grounded in it,
Affures the heart and pacifies the fpirit:

To them that loue and reuerence his name
Profperity betides, and want of fhame.

Thus can no tyrant pull them from the hands
Of mighty God, that for their fafety ftands,
Who euer fees, and euer can defend :
Them whom he loues he loues vnto the end.

So that the more their furie ouerfloweth,
The more eche on his owne deftruction foweth ;
And as they ftriue with God in pollicie,
So are they fooner brought to miferie.

Like as the fauage boar, diflodge from den
And hotely chafed by purfuit of men,
Runnes furioufly on them that come him neare,
And goares him felfe vpon the hunters fpeare.

The gentle puiffant Lamb, their champion bold,
So helps to conquer all that hurt his fold,
That quickly they and all their progenie
Confounded are, and brought to miferie.

This is of Juda the couragious Lion,
The conquering Captaine, and the Rocke of Sion,
Whofe fauour is as great to Jacobs line,
As is his fearfull frowne to Philiftine.

FINIS.   T. B.

Printed at London by A. Iflip. 1597.

Salomons Housewife,

OR THE PRAISE OF A GOOD WIFE, AS SET FORTH IN
HIS PROVERBS.

*Who can finde a vertuous woman, her price is
aboue rubies.*—Prov.

E that a gratious wife doth finde,
　　Whofe life puts vertue chiefe in ure,
One of the right good houfwife kinde,
　　That man may well him felfe affure,
And boafting fay that he hath found
The richeft treafure on the ground :

Whoso enioyeth such a loue,
　　Let him resolue with harts content,
She euer constantly will proue
　　A carefull nurse and want prevent;
With diligence and carefull heede,
Preuenting tast of beggers neede.

And while she liues she will procure,
　　By true and faithfull industrie,
Tencrease his wealth, and to insure
　　His state in all securitie:
To seeke his quiet, worke his ease,
And for a word no way displease.

Her houshold folke from sloth to keepe
　　She will indeuour with good heede;
At worke more wakefull then asleepe,
　　With place and stuffe which houswifes neede
To be employde: her hands also
The way to worke will others show.

Her wit a common wealth maintaines
　　Of needments for her houshold store,
And, like a ship, herselfe containes
　　The riches brought from forraine shore
Arriuing, with a bounteous hand,
Dispearsing treasure through the land.

Before the day she will arise
    To order things, and to prouide
What may her family suffise,
    That they at labour may abide.
If she haue land, no paines shall want
To purchase vines, set, sow and plant.

No honest labour shele omit
    In aught she can attaine vnto,
But will essay with strength and wit,
    Adding the utmost she can doe;
And if the profit comes about,
By night her candle goeth not out.

A willing hand to the distrest
    She lends, and is a cheerfull giuer:
Come winters cold and frostie guest,
    When idle housfwifes quake and quiuer,
She and her houshold cloathed well,
The weathers hardnesse do expell.

Her skill doth worke faire tapestry,
    With linnen furnisht of the best:
Her needle workes doe beautifie,
    And she in costly skarlet drest:
When senators assembled bee
Her husbands honour there shele see.

Her spinning shall her store increase;
    The finest cloath shall yeeld her gaine,
And daily profit shall not cease,
    Which her vnidle hands maintaine.
Her cloathing shall her worth expresse,
And honours yeares her end possesse.

Her mouth shall neuer opened bee,
    But wisedome will proceede from it;
And such milde gratious wordes yeelds she,
    Sweetnesse vpon her tong doth sit.
In age she will her care addresse
To eate no bread of idlenesse.

Her children shall their duty show
    Most reuerent to her all her life,
Her husband blesse that he did know
    The time to meete with such a wife;
And vttering foorth his happinesse,
Her vertues in this wife expresse.

I know tis true that more then one
    Good housewife there is to be found,
But I may boast that thou alone
    Aboue all women dost abound:
Yea, I protest in all my dayes
Thou art the first, and this thy praise.

What thing is fauour but a shade?
    It hath no certaine lasting hower;
Whereof is wanton beautie made,
    That withereth like a sommers flower?
When these shall end their date of dayes,
She that feares God shall liue with prayse.

And such a wife of worthie woorth,
    Due glories lot will to her fall,
And great assemblies will giue foorth
    What vertues shees adornd withall:
Her lifes renowme to fame shall reach,
Her good example others teach.

May batchelors of each degree,
    In choosing of a beauteous wife,
Remember, what is ioy to see
    May lead to wofulnesse and strife:
Beauty is not a braue outside;
Beauty within is beauty's pride.

T. D.

FINIS.

Printed for the Assignes of T. Simcocke.

The Story of Ill May-day

In the time of King Henry viij, and why it was fo called:
and how Queene Katherine begged the Liues of
two thoufand London Prentices.

To the tune of Effex good night.

———o———

PERUSE the ftory of this land,
    and with aduifement note the fame,
And you fhall iuftly vnderftand
    how Ill May-day firft got the name:
For when King Henry th'eight did raigne,
    and rulde our famous kingdome here,
His royall Queene he had from Spaine,
    with whome he liude full many a yere.

Queene Katherine, as our ſtories tell,
    ſometime had beene his brothers wife,
By which vnlawfull marriage fell
    an endleſſe trouble during life :
But ſuch kinde loue he ſtill conceiude
    of his good Queene and all her friends,
It was in Spaine and France perceiude,
    and hither all their journey tends.

They with good leaue were ſuffered
    within our noble realme to ſtay ;
Which multitude made victual deare,
    and all things els from day to day :
For ſtrangers then did ſo increaſe,
    by reaſon of King Henries Queene,
And all were priuiledgde in peace
    to dwell in London, as was ſeene.

Our tradeſmen had ſmall dealing then,
    and who but ſtrangers bore the bell ;
Which was a griefe to Engliſh men,
    to ſee them here in London dwell.
Wherefore, God wot, on May-day eue,
    as prentices on maying went,
They made the magiſtrates beleeue
    they had no other bad intent.

But ſuch a may-game it was knowne,
    the like in London neuer were ;
For by the ſame full many a one
    with loſſe of life did pay full deere :

Then thousands came with Bilbo blade,
    as with an army they should meete,
And such a bloudy slaughter made
    of straungers as fillde all the streete,

And made the channels run with blood
    in euery streete where they remainde ;
Yea, euery one in danger stood
    that any of their part maintainde.
The rich, the poore, the olde, the yong,
    beyond the seas if born and bred,
By prentices there suffred wrong
    when armed thus they gatherd head.

Such multitudes together went,
    no warlike troopes could them withstand,
Nor yet by pollicy preuent
    what they by force thus tooke in hand :
Till at the last King Henries power
    this multitude had compast round,
And with the strength of Londons Tower
    they were by force suppreft and bound.

Hundreds were hangd by martial law
    on sign posts at their masters doores,
By which the rest were kept in awe,
    and frighted from such lewd vproars.
Some others who their fact repented,
    two thousand prentices at least,
Were all before the king presented,
    as Maior and magistrates thought best.

The Story of ill May-day.

And two and two together tyde,
    through Temple Bar and Strand they goe
To Weſtminſter there to be tryde,
    with ropes about their neckes alſo :
But ſuch a crye in euery ſtreete
    till then was neuer heard nor knowne,
By mothers for their children ſweete
    vnhappily thus ouerthrowne.

Their bitter moanes and ſad laments
    did reach the Court and places neare,
Whereat the Queene her ſelfe relents,
    though it concernd her countrey deare.
What if, quoth ſhee, by Spaniſh blood
    haue Londons ſtately ſtreetes beene wet,
Yet will I ſeeke faire Englands good,
    and pardon for theſe young men get.

Or els the world will ſpeake of mee,
    and ſay Queene Katherine was vnkind,
And iudge me ſtill the cauſe to bee
    theſe young men did misfortune finde
And ſo, diſrobde of rich attires,
    with haire hangd downe, ſhe ſadly hies,
And of her gracious Lord requires
    a boone, which hardly he denyes.

The liues, quoth ſhe, of all the bloomes
    yet budding greene, theſe youths, I craue :
O ! let them not haue timeleſſe tombes,
    for Nature longer limit gaue.

In faying fo the pearly teares
    fell trickling from her princely eies ;
Whereat his gentle Queene he cheares,
    and fays, Stand vp ! fweete Lady, rife.

The liues of them I freelie giue,
    no man this kindneffe fhall debar :
Thou haft thy boone, and they may liue
    to ferue me in my Bullein warre.
No fooner was this pardon giuen,
    but peales of ioy rung through the hall,
As though it thunderd downe from heauen
    the Queenes renowne amongft them all.

For which, kinde Queene, with ioyfull hart,
    fhee gaue to them both thankes & praife ;
And fo from them did gently part,
    and liude beloued all her dayes.
And when King Henry ftood in neede
    of trufty fouldiers at command,
Thefe prentices prou'de men indeede,
    and feard no force of warlike band.

For at the fiedge of Tours in France
    they fhewd them felues braue Englifh men ;
At Bullein alfo did aduance
    S. Georges glorious Standard then.
Let Turwen, Turney, and thofe townes
    that good King Henry nobly wonne,
Tell London prentices renownes,
    and all the deedes by them there donne.

Thus Ill May-day, and ill May games,
  performde in young and tender dayes,
Can be no let to all their fames,
  or ftaines of manhood any wayes :
But now it is ordained by law,
  we fee, on May-day Eue at night,
To keepe vnruly youths in awe,
  our Londons Watch in armour bright :

Still to preuent the like mifdeed
  which once by head-ftrong young men came ;
And thats the caufe, as I doe reade,
  May-day hath got fo ill a name.
So now henceforth we need to feare
  no fuch mifhap as they did bring,
But peace and order euerie where,
  and loyal harts vnto our King.

London.   Printed for Thomas Goffon.

The desperate Damsells Tragedy,
OR THE FAITHLESSE YOUNG MAN.
To the tune of Dulcina.

———o———

N the gallant month of June,
When sweet rofes are in prime,
And each bird with feuerall tune
Harmoniously falutes the time,

   then to delight
   my appetite
I walkt into a meddow faire,
   and in the fhade
   I fpyed a maide,
Whofe loue had brought her to difpaire.

Shee her hands fate fadly wringing,
Making piteous exclamation,
Vpon a falfe young man for bringing
Her into this great vexation.
   Quoth fhe, falfe youth,
   Is there no truth
In thee, of faith haft thou no fhare?
   no, thou haft none,
   tis to well knowne,
For me, poore wretch, now in defpaire.

How oftentimes haft thou protefted
That thou loueft me well indeed?
And I performed what was requefted:
Too much truft my woe doth breed.
   I let thee haue
   what thou didft craue,
Seduced by thy fpeeches faire;
   and hauing had
   thy will, falfe lad,
At laft thou leau'ft me in defpaire.

My deareft iewell thou haft taken,
Which fhould ftand me in great ftead,

And now thou haſt me quite forſaken,
And art, like falſe Æneas, fled
    from Dido true:
    what can inſue
This faithles deed? but end my care:
    like her, a knife
    muſt end my life,
For I, like her, am in deſpaire.

Then, ſith tis ſo, come, gentle death,
I yeeld my ſelfe vnto thy power,
Moſt willing to reſigne my breath
I am this inſtant time and howre:
    let thy keene dart
    ſuch force impart
That I may die, oh! do not ſpare:
    from earth I came,
    and willing am
Hence to returne with grim deſpaire.

When ſhe theſe bitter words had ſpoken
From her minde ſo fraught with woe,
Her heart was in her boſome broken.
Teares aboundantly did flow
    from her faire eyes;
    then to the ſkies
She did direct her hands with prayer,
    and ſeem'd to moue
    the pow'rs aboue
To ſcourge the cauſe of her deſpaire.

THE SECOND PART. *To the fame tune.*

You Gods (quoth fhe) I inuocate,
That as your iudgements ftill are iuft,
My wrongs, I pray you, vindicate.
Oh, may no mayds that young man truft!
   henceforth may he
   fo wretched be,
That none for him at all fhall care,
   but that he may
   for his foule play
Be brought, like me, to grim defpaire.

Hauing made an end of praying,
Suddenly fhe drew a knife,
And I, that neere vnfeene was ftaying,
Ran in haft to faue her life;
   but ere that I
   to her could cry,
That her owne life fhe might forbeare,
   fhee, Dido like,
   her heart did ftrike:
Thus dyde the damfell in defpaire.

With fuch force her felfe fhe ftabbed,
Blood ranne out abundantly:
My heart within my bofome throbbed
To behold this tragedy.
   Yet though fhe bled,
   fhe was fcarce dead,

But gasping lay with her last ayre,
     and vnto me
     shee spake words three,
Which shewed the cause of her despaire.

Sir (quoth she) muse not to see me
Desperatly my selfe to slay,
For this fatall stroake doth free me
From disgrace another way.
     My honours dead,
     my credits fledd,
Why therefore should I liue in care?
     this being spoke,
     her heart strings broke:
Thus dyed the damsell in despaire.

When death had done his worst vnto her,
I did wishtly on her looke,
And by her fauour I did know her:
Therefore I my journey tooke
     vnto the towne
     where shee was knowne,
And to her friends I did declare
     what dismall fate
     had hapt of late
Vnto this damsell in despaire.

With brinish teares her friends lamented
To heare of her timelesse end,
And euery one in griefe consented,
And with me along did wend

    vnto the place
   where lay that face
That late aliue was fresh and faire,
    now wanne and pale,
    caufe life did faile :
Her life fhe ended in defpaire.

When this was told to her falfe louer,
He was of his wits beftraught,
And wildly ran the country ouer ;
Home hee'd by no meanes be brought.
    Let this tale then
    warne all young men
Vnconftancy ftill to forbeare,
    for he betraide
    this harmeleffe mayde
Vnto her death through grim defpaire.

    FINIS.   *M. P.*

   London.   Printed for H. G.
     1627.

Mans Creation, Adams Fall, and Christs Redemption.

In this Table is set forth three principall things:
First, mans Creation: secondly, Adams Fall:
and, lastly, the happy restoring againe
of all the faithfull by Christ to the
vnchangeable loue of God.

A Table fit for all Christians to know.

―――o―――

ALMIGHTIE God made by his Word
All creatures that the earth afford:
The dark and light was then divided,
And thus by God it was decided.
The light by him was called Day,
The darknesse Night, and so they stay.

2.
And God faw all, and it was good,
From man to beaft and fruitfull bud :
But Enuie then did Eue beguile,
And Eue brought Adam to exile
By eating that which was fore-told,
That they with it fhould not be bold.

3.
Soone after this God did appeare,
Then Eue and Adam did him feare;
And as He walk'd in coole of day
Thofe finners hid themfelues away;
But God did call them here below,
To tell him how they came to know.

4.
Thus then begins the Man to fay,
She whom thou gau'ft did I obay;
And Eue likewife excus'de the fact,
Imputing it to Serpents act.
And thus doe moft, in Adams line,
Shame not to fay, *The fault's not mine.*

5.
But let all thofe thinke thus withall;
That God is free from Adams fall,
Elfe how could he in truth proceede
Againft our Parents, as we reade?
He hates iniuftice here below,
And this his righteoufneffe doth show.

6.

Now, when our Parents tale was done,
Then iuſtly God proceedes vpon :
The Serpent firſt he curſt in place,
And made Eue ſubiect with diſgrace ;
And man in ſorrow labour muſt
All dayes of life, then turne to duſt.

7.

And Death likewiſe the time shall rue,
For Chriſt alone shall it ſubdue :
This truth is knowne to Satans woe,
Since Chriſt hath broke his head alſo ;
For God did promiſe make to ſend
A godly ſeede, all ſtrife to end.

8.

This Seede is Chriſt, free from all ſinne :
What Adam loſt, that Hee did winne
By keeping that without all blame,
Which neuer man could doe the ſame ;
And in our ſtead he paid our debt,
To ſet vs free from Satans net.

9.

God will not now, nor e'er hereafter,
Condemne vs for our ſinnes by nature ;
For how can that with iuſtice ſtand,
When God ſhall twice one debt demand ?
Therefore, it now remaines with vs
That we beleeue Chriſt hath done thus.

10

And thus beleeuing faithfully,
Chrifts righteoufneffe we muft apply;
For when we haue done all we may,
On his obedience muft wee ftay,
And thofe whofe faith is found and true
Doe practife ftill Gods lawes to doe.

11.

Of fuch as thefe doth God with fpeede
Accept their will as for their deede,
And though they finne, for fo doe all,
Yet finally they fhall not fall;
For by beleife in Chrift aboue
None can remoue thefe from his loue.

12.

O! loue vs then of thy free grace,
Whereby in heauen we may haue place,
To praife thee ftill for thy free loue,
And loue thy praife for e'er aboue.
And now, good Lord, we craue no more,
But loue vs for thy loue therefore.

FINIS.   *I. D.*

Printed at London for Thomas Ellis, at the figne of the Chriftopher in Pauls Church yard. 1629.

The Honor of the Inns of Court Gentlemen,

Or a briefe recitall of the Magnificent and Matchleffe Show, that paffed from Hatton and Ely houfe in Holborne to Whitehall, on Monday night being the third of February, and the next day after Candlemas.

To the tune of our noble King in his Progreffe.

Y noble Muſe, aſſiſt mee,
    that I may with credit
      vndergoe the taſke.
A humor hath poſſeſt mee
    To write a new ditty
of the triumphant Maſke,
Which lately was performed
    in high magnifique ſort,
To the honor of thoſe gentry
    that liue at the Inns of Court.

Theſe noble minded gallants,
    to ſhew their true loue
      to our Royall King and Queene,
Did largely ſpend their talents
To make a faire ſhew,
    that the like was neuer ſeene.
To ſet downe all exactly
    my ſkil comes far too ſhort,
To the honor of thoſe gentry
    that liue at the Inns of Court.

The next day after Candlemas,
    betwixt the houres
      of ſeuen and nine at night,
This ſtately company did paſſe
From Hatton-houſe in Holborne
    vnto White-hall in ſight:
Of ſuch a peereleſſe obiect
    no age can make report,

To the honour of thofe gentry
    that liue at the Inns of Court.

A various crew of anticks all,
    which feuerall humors
    in fhape did reprefent,
The number of them was not fmall,
Which to the fpectators
    gaue wonderful content :
Each one in his due pofture
    did fhew exceeding fport,
To the honor of thofe gentry
    that liue at the Inns of Court.

A hundred fweet yong gentlemen,
    that all vpon great horfes
    were mounted gallantly,
Clad in white cloath of tiffue then,
And red and white feathers,
    moft glorious to the eye ;
In equipage moft fumptuous
    they paft in folemne fort :
Thefe were the braue young gentry
    that liue at the Inns of Court.

By two and two, and foure by foure,
    they flowly did ride
    on their proud and haughty fteeds :
Search all the lands in Europe ore,
No men, both in perfon
    and face thefe men exceeds.

Their time was long in paſſing,
    yet people thought 'twas ſhort,
So much they prays'd the gentry
    that liue at the Inns of Court.

The drums and trumpets loudly
    did found before
    this heroick company :
The horſes danced as proudly,
As ſenſible
    of this high ſolemnity.
Their fortune did attend them
    in braue and ſolemne ſort,
To the honour of thoſe gentry
    that liue at the Inns of Court.

THE SECOND PART. *To the ſame tune.*

But that which admiration
    exacts from all men
    which ſaw or heard of it
Was the charets
Which in faſhion
    for mighty princes and conquerors moſt fit :
The glory of this action
    exceedeth all report,
To the honour of thoſe gentry
    that liue at the Innes of Court.

And fixe there were in number :
    in thoſe the maſkers

themfelues did fit in ftate,
Which made the people wonder,
And rauifhed the fenfes
    of all that there did waite.
The oldeft man aliue
    cannot the like report,
To the honour of thofe gentry
    that liue at the Innes of Court.

Two charets had foure horfes each,
    that went by two and two:
    the reft did goe by foure a breaft,
In order without any breach:
A thing which of all things
    becomes a triumph beft;
No one did breake aray,
    but went in fober fort,
To the honour of thofe gentry
    that liue at the Innes of Court.

Our gracious King, with his deare Queene,
    did fit to behold
    this fo beautiful fhow:
It ioy'd their hearts when they had feene
The true and loyal loue
    that their fubiects to them owe.
Vnto their long liu'd credit
    they fhewd their princely fport,
To the honour of thofe gentry
    that liue at the Innes of Court.

Many thoufand pounds of gold, tis thought,
    hath not the charge
      of this matchleffe mafke defrayd ;
Yet let no critick deeme that naught
Which hath on a fudden
      employ'd fo many a trade.
Young people may hereafter
    vnto their young report
The honour of thofe gentry
      that liue at the Innes of Court.

No prince throughout al Chriftendom
    can like to our King
      of fo ftrange a triumph boaft :
Thofe ftrangers that doe hither come
Wil fpread our Ilands glory
      abroad in many a coaft ;
For al their quaint deuifes
    to this muft come farre fhort,
To the honour of thofe gentry
      that liue at the Innes of Court.

FINIS.

M. P.

London. Printed for Thomas Lambert.

An Excellent Medley

Which you may admire at (without offence)
For euery line speaks a contrary sense.

The tune is Tarleton's Medley.

———o———

N summer time when folks make hay,
All is not true that people say;
The fool's the wisest in the play,
     tush! take away your hand.

The fidlers boy hath broke his bafe,
Sirs, is not this a pitious cafe?
Moft gallants loath to fmell the mace
    of Wood-ftreet.

The City follows courtly pride;
Jone fwears fhe cannot John abide,
Dick wears a dagger by his fide :
    come, tell us what's to pay.
The lawyers thriue by others fall,
The weakeft always goes to the wall,
The fhoo-maker commandeth all
    at's pleafure.

The weauer prays for hufwiues ftore,
A pretty woman was Jane Shore,
Kick the bafe rafcal out o' the door,
    peace, peace, you brawling curs!
A cuckolds band wears out behind,
Tis eafie to beguile the blind,
All people are not of one mind,
    hold, carman!

Our women cut their hair like men,
The cock's ore-mafter'd by the hen;
Theres hardly one good friend in ten :
    turn there on the right hand.
But few regard the cries o' th' poor,
Will fpendeth all [and fomething more]
The fouldier longeth to go o're,
    braue knocking!

What shall we do in these sad days?
Will not the wicked mend their waies?
Some lose their liues in drunken frays;
    the pudding burns to th' pot.
The cooper says the tubs [hold grift,]
The cobler preaches what he lift,
Their knauery now is manifest;
    hold, halter!

When the fifth Harry sail'd to France:
Let me alone for a country dance,
Nell will bewail her lucklefs chance,
    fie on falfe-hearted men!
Dick Tarleton was a merry wag:
Hark how that prating afs doth brag,
John Dory fold his ambling nag
    for kick-fhaws.

The faylor counts the fhip his houfe,
I'le fay no more but Dun's the moufe,
He is no man that fcorns a loufe;
    vain pride vndoes the land.
Hard-hearted men make corn fo dear,
Few Frenchmen loue well Englifh bear;
I hope e're long good news to hear,
    hey luftick!

Now hides are cheap the tanner thriues:
Hang thofe bafe knaues that beat their wiues,
He needs muft go that the Deuil driues,
    God blefs us from a gun!

The beadles make the lame to run,
Vaunt not before the battel's won,
A cloud fometimes may hide the fun:
    chance medley.

The furgeon thriues by fencing fchools,
Some for ftrong liquor pawn their tools,
For one wife man there's twenty fools:
    oh! when fhall we be married?
In time of youth when I was wild,
Who toucheth pitch fhall be defil'd,
Mol is afraid fhe is with child:
    peace, Peter!

The poor ftill hope for better days,
I do not loue thefe long delays;
All loue and charity decaies,
    in the daies of old.
Im very loath to pawn my cloak,
Meer pouerty doth me prouoke;
They fay a fcald head is foon broke,
    poor trading!

Hark, mother, hark, there's news in town.
What tell you me of half a crown?
Now the Excife is going down,
    thou prateft like an afs.
I fcorn the coyn, giue me the man:

Pray pledge the health, fir ; I began :
I loue King Charles, fay what you can,
 God faue him !

The Dutchmen thriue by fea and land,
Women are fhips and muft be man'd,
Lets brauely to our colours ftand,
 Courage, my hearts of gold !
I read in modern hiftories
The King of Sweden's victories :
At Iflington there's pudding pies,
 hot cuftards.

The tapfter is vndone by chalk.
Tush ! tis in vain to prate and talk,
The parrot prattles ; walk, knaues, walk.
 Duke Humfrey lies in Pauls.
The fouldier hath but fmall regard,
There's weekly news in Pauls Church Yard :
The poor man crys the world goes hard,
 cold winter !

Heigh for New England, hoyfe vp fail !
The truth is ftrong and will preuail,
Fill me a cup of nappy ale,
 hang care ! the kings a comming.
This egg hath long a hatching been :
When you haue done, then wee'l begin,
Oh, what an age do we liue in !
 hang pinching.

From Long-lane cloath and Turn-ſtile boots,
O, fie vpon theſe ſcabbed coots!
The cheapeſt meat is reddish roots,
    come all for a penny.
Light my tobacco quickly here.
There lies a pretty woman near:
This boy will come to naught, I fear,
    proud coxcombe!

The world is full of odious ſins,
'Tis ten to one but this horſe wins:
Fools ſet ſtools to break wiſe mens shins;
    this man's more knaue then fool.
Jane oft in priuate meets with Tom.
Husband, thouart kindly welcome home,
Haſt any money? lend me ſome,
    I'me broken.

In antient times all things were cheap,
'Tis good to look before you leap,
When corn is ripe 'tis time to reap:
    once walking by the way.
A jealous man the cuckow loaths,
The gallant compliments with oaths,
A wench will make you ſell your cloaths;
    run, broker.

The courtier and the country man;
Let's liue as honeſt as we can:

When Arthur firſt in court began,
    his men wore hanging ſleeues.
In May when graſs and flowers are green,
The ſtrangeſt ſight that ere was ſeen.
God ſend our gracious King and Queen
    to London!

FINIS.   *M. P.*

Printed at London for H. G.

NOTES.

PAGE 1. Two propernue Ballettes. Neither date nor printer's name are appended to the broadfide containing thefe two firft Ballads; but the typography is obvioufly early, and they may be affigned to fome year between 1530 and 1540—older, we apprehend, than the most ancient printed ballad the date of which has been afcertained.

P. 6. Hugh Syngelton, the printer of this broadfide, was carrying on his trade about the year 1550; his firft known work bears date 1553. Our fpecimen once formed the fly-leaf of a book, and part of the text is deftroyed.

P. 8. This ballad was communicated to the editor by the late Dr. Maitland, at the time he was librarian to the Archbifhop of Canterbury. Under the imprint is placed the figure of Robert Copeland, as it appears on the title-pages of fome of the other productions of his prefs. Dr. Maitland, at the fame time, ftated to the editor that there exifted, in one of the Lambeth MSS., another copy with fome variations: although it refembles the ftyle of Skelton's "Now a dayes," (Works, i, p. 148), it has no name, nor initials, either to the printed or to the written copy.

P. 16. Refpecting John Pit, or Pitts, fee "Bibliographical Account," etc. ii, 172.

P. 21. Throgmorton was hanged, not beheaded as might be fuppofed from the wood-cut. The fame wood-cut was ufed in 1641 on the title-page to a profe narrative of the death of Strafford, and for other fimilar productions, in profe and verfe: at the earlieft date, at which we have met with it, it had been much battered.

P. 28. We have no means of affigning to their real owner the initials W. M. at the end of this broadfide, but the fame letters follow fome commendatory lines prefixed to F. Twyne's "News from the North", 1579 and 1582. There were two editions of this ballad in the fame year, differing only verbally, though fome of the changes are curious. One edition, probably the firft, was reprinted in "Roxburghe Ballads", 1847, and the other is here given.

P. 29. The initials at the end of this elegiac poem are thofe of Richard Mulcafter; and he may have compofed what is by no means a difcreditable piece of verfification.

P. 31. The late Mr. Lemon, of the State Paper Office, gave the editor a copy of this droll and not ill-written ballad. It feems that the Society of Antiquaries has a proof of it, which contains a ftanza more than the examplar we have employed. The editor has alfo an old MS. of it, differing materially from both. It has no date, and the wood-cuts, both at the beginning and end, are not fo old as the typography: yet the knight on horfeback has the Tudor rofe very obvioufly embroidered on the houfings of his fteed. We have feen it prefixed to old ballads of "Patient Griffell," publifhed as late as 1640 or 1650.

P. 36. The place given to this head, on the broadfide to which it belongs, feems to fhew that it was intended for a likenefs of Young Babbington, who was fo dangeroufly energetic in the aid he attempted to give to the Queen of Scots: if fo, it is, we apprehend, the only exifting reprefentation of his features. It was not given in 1840, when this ballad was firft reprinted.

P. 41. The initials T. D. fhew that this broadfide was by Thomas Deloney, "the ballading filk-weaver", who generally availed himfelf of public executions in order to profit by the occasion. We may notice here, that the registers of St. Giles Cripplegate shew that he resided in that parish, where his son Richard was christened on 16th October, 1586, the year of our ballad, and about a month after the execution therein commemorated.

P. 42. From Thomas Nash, we learn that Philip Stubbes, the author of this ballad (taken by Wright from an undated tract), was one of "the common pamphleters of London"; and, apparently by way of derision, Nash couples him with Deloney and Armin. Unquestionably, the versification of the piece before us has very humble pretensions to be called poetry: it is subscribed P. S. in the broadside, and not at length as in the tract, which contains another ballad by Stubbes.

P. 48. The most remarkable circumstance about this ballad is that it is in part founded upon the main incident in Shakespeare's "Merchant of Venice"; while "Cymbeline" (unless the ballad be older, which hardly seems probable) is laid under contribution for another important circumstance. The conclusion, as regards the Green Knight, was probably derived from romance: Green Knights are mentioned both by Gascoigne and Warner. The original B. L., without printer's name, formerly passed through the hands of Thorpe, the bookseller; and the editor has a much corrupted copy of it, "Printed and sold in Aldermary Church-yard, Bow Lane, London," n. d.

P. 57. The two heads seem intended for likenesses of the man (a disguised Jesuit) who escaped from Bridewell, and of the woman who assisted him; they are in a separate frame, as if to distinguish them, especially, from the other twelve culprits. There is no name and no initials at the end of the ballad

P. 63. Mr. Page of Plymouth was murdered by his wife, her paramour, and their accomplices, in February 1591, and they were executed at Barnſtaple very ſoon afterwards; about which date this and the two enſuing ballads muſt have been printed. The whole ſtory may be read in Vol. II of the "Shakeſpeare Society's Papers", p. 79; and the remembrance of it continued ſo fresh in 1599, that Ben Jonſon and Dekker were then employed upon a tragedy containing the incidents. See Henslowe's Diary, p. 155, etc.

P. 73. "The Weaver's Song" was probably firſt printed in Deloney's "Jack of Newbury", of which the earlieſt notice ſeems to have been in 1595. From "Jack of Newbury" it was tranſplanted into a broadſide, no doubt on account of its popularity.

P. 76. Henry Harper, whoſe name is found at the end of this broadſide, was a publiſher of ballads and chap-books as late as 1640 or 1650; but this animated hiſtorical effuſion muſt have been very current before 1600, becauſe it is quoted in Heywood's play of "The firſt part of Edward IV", of that date, Aɛt II, ſc. 2.

P. 79. There is a copy of this ballad in the British Muſeum, but of an edition different from the preſent, and with different ornamentation: we ſuſpeɛt that R. I. [Richard Jones], whoſe initials, as printer, are at the end of the copy we have uſed, pirated it with ſome variations from Edward White's firſt edition, which has T. D. at the termination, as the initials of Deloney, the author. R. I. did not venture to repeat T. D., and indeed did not avow his own name at length in connexion with the broadſide, which he headed by a ſhip-of-war in full ſail. The copy in the B. M. has no ſhip of war above the title.

P. 87. The letters T. B. at the end of this moral and

religious broadside are thofe of Thomas Beard, author of the "Theatre of God's Judgments", 4to., 1597. We had a MS. copy of the performance in our hands for many years, not knowing from whence it was derived, until we met with it a fhort time ago in the firft edition of Beard's work.

P. 91. By Deloney; originally publifhed as a broadfide, and afterwards included in a volume called "Strange Hiftories" in 1607. The differences between the two copies are not of much importance, excepting that the concluding ftanza, one of the beft, was omitted in 1607. Simcocke, no doubt, reprinted from an earlier copy, which had the whole ballad as it came from the pen of its author.

P. 96. Also in "Strange Hiftories", 1607, but without the concluding quatrain, fo that it is there imperfect, the laft ftanza having only four inftead of eight lines. No doubt, when the broadfide firft came out, Queen Elizabeth was reigning, and was celebrated at the clofe: this portion was omitted in 1607, becaufe King James was then on the throne; but when Goffon reprinted the ballad, about 1630 or 1640, he made the conclufion complimentary to Charles I. No copy is known which contains the original tribute to Elizabeth, and which muft have appeared about 1597 or 1598.

P. 102. The initials at the end prove that this production was by Martin Parker, and the date shews that it must have been his earlieft effort. It has nowhere been affigned to him, or even noticed, that we are aware of.

P. 108. By John Davies of Hereford, as we gather from his initials at the clofe. His earlieft effufion was a fonnet to W. Parry, printed on the last page of his account (4to., 1600) of the voyage of the Shirleys: Parry's tract is fo

S

rare, in confequence of the order againſt it at Stationers' Hall (fee Pref. p. xii), that it has not been recorded by fome modern bibliographers: it was reprinted by the prefent editor a few years fince. The fonnet by Davies occupies the laſt leaf.

P. 112. The proceffion which this ballad celebrates was for Shirley's Masque "The Triumph of Peace," performed at Whitehall on 3rd February, 1633. The ballad was one of Martin Parker's temporary effufions; and it was unknown to the Rev. Mr. Dyce when he completed Gifford's edition of Shirley's Works: it has not been included in any liſt of M. P.'s publications.

P. 118. We have never met with a fpecimen of a "Medley" in any ancient or modern collection of ballads; yet, from the time of Tarleton downwards, they were extremely popular, and the tune to which "Tarleton's Medley" (now loſt) was fung was generally, as here, adopted by his imitators. One of the moſt succefsful was by the writer of this ballad, which contains the prominent lines of many popular performances, not a few of which will inſtantly occur to memory; fuch as "In fummer time", "A pretty woman was Jane Shore," "Dick Tarleton was a merry wag," "When our fifth Harry fail'd for France," "John Dory fold his ambling nag," "When Arthur firſt in court began," etc., etc. The fac-fimile of a ſtreet-mufician at the head of this reprint, gives an exact and contemporaneous reprefentation of the cumbrous "Lincolnſhire bagpipe", the "melancholy drone" of which is celebrated by Shakefpeare, Henry IV, Part I, Act I, fc. 2.

FINIS.

www.ingramcontent.com/pod-product-compliance
Lightning Source LLC
Chambersburg PA
CBHW030343170426
43202CB00010B/1224